IMAGES
of America

LAWRENCE
VOLUME II

FRANK LESLIE'S ILLUSTRATED NEWSPAPER

Entered according to Act of Congress, in the year 1889, by the JUDGE PUBLISHING COMPANY, in the Office of the Librarian of Congress at Washington.—Entered at the Post-office, New York, N. Y., as Second-class Matter.

No. 1771.—Vol. LXIX.]   NEW YORK—FOR THE WEEK ENDING AUGUST 24, 1889.   [PRICE, 10 CENTS. $4.00 YEARLY. 13 WEEKS, $1.00.

President Benjamin Harrison is shown here arriving in Lawrence during the first year of his presidency (1889).

IMAGES
of America

LAWRENCE
VOLUME II

Ken Skulski

ARCADIA

First published 1997
Copyright © Immigrant City Archives, 1997

ISBN 0 7524 0803-8

Published by Arcadia Publishing,
an imprint of the Chalford Publishing Corporation,
One Washington Center, Dover, New Hampshire 03820.
Printed in Great Britain

Library of Congress Cataloging-in-Publication Data applied for

For Yvette and Peter Skulski

A balloon ascension was photographed on the North Common *c.* 1890.

Contents

MANY NATIONALITIES
MANY LANGUAGES
ONE COUNTRY

ALL THE WORLD HAS COME TO LAWRENCE

This celebration of ethnic heritage was sponsored by the International Institute of Lawrence in the Everett Mill on Union Street in 1936. Ilona Korziuk Volungus (right) models a Polish costume while Olga Galushka (left), a crafts instructor for the institute, is in Russian garb.

FRONT COVER ILLUSTRATION: James N. Gurdy, an Essex Street baker and confectioner, began manufacturing his immensely popular Jersey Ice Cream around 1904 at 9 Amesbury Street near the state armory. Not long after, the company established facilities off Water Street where it is believed this photograph was taken. The picture shows one of the first motorized vehicles used by the company for local deliveries. Neither of these two people are identified. By the 1920s, Jersey Ice Cream was sold all over the East Coast.

Introduction

On April 17, 1847, following much objection and lawlessness, the pioneer townsfolk of Lawrence were finally recognized in a charter signed by the governor of the commonwealth.

Lawrence was fast becoming a boom town. The population was already in excess of three thousand persons, nearly one third of whom were poor, Irish immigrants residing in "shantees" on either side of the Merrimack River. A devastating famine in Ireland forced many of these unskilled, unschooled, Roman Catholic émigrés to this largely undeveloped land. By February of 1847, ninety shanties housed most of the Irish tenants. Irish workers received between 50¢ and 75¢ a day for backbreaking work, half as much as a skilled Yankee could earn. Typhus, dysentery, and tuberculosis were the major causes of death in Lawrence. Cheap Irish labor contributed significantly to the construction of the Great Stone Dam, the North Canal, and most of the early textile mills. It was not uncommon for recent Irish arrivals in Boston to walk the distance to Lawrence, as few could afford either the train or coach.

The town's first extensive human tragedy occurred in October of 1847. Two men employed by the Essex Company in construction of a coffer dam were drowned when the structure collapsed. One of these was a recent immigrant. Many more were seriously injured. That winter, five days before Christmas, an attempt was made to break into the Essex Company's safe. Lawrence then was as much a pioneer town as any frontier town out west. In 1878 Lawrence historian Robert H. Tewksbury recalled that besides the industrious and hardworking came "unfortunates, speculators, quacks and pretenders."

Among the immigrants laboring here in these early years was a young German named Henry Wirz. By 1864 he became, for many, the most hated man in America. Wirz was then commandant of the notorious Andersonville Prison in Georgia where upwards of two hundred Union soldiers died daily. Lawrence attracted the best and shed the worst.

During the winter of 1846–47, the Essex Company's agent wrote: "Soon after we began to collect here we found law wanting; next, churches and a school; next, the enforcement of law was wanted, and we had constables appointed. Now the law issues its warrant, the constables arrest, but the prisoner escapes for want of a jail. . . . The various trades are already well represented here. We have constant applications and correspondence relating to business openings; among others, one wishes to know if he can have a monopoly on the coffin trade in the new town."

This new town did not emerge without controversy. When the Essex Company petitioned the commonwealth for the establishment of the municipality that would incorporate lands from both Andover and Methuen, the residents of these two bordering towns were not universally in accord. Protests were loud and vehement, especially from the Methuen side. Citing concern in a January remonstrance, they complained that a "large foreign and pauper population . . . will be thrown upon said town." But the legislature rejected their pleas.

Yet another issue was that of a suitable name for this new town. Since October of 1846 the little post office on the corner of Turnpike (now Broadway) and Common Streets, which also housed the police station, used the name of "Merrimack." This was but one of numerous appellations in popular use. Charles Storrow of the Essex Company wanted the town called "Lawrence" after Abbott Lawrence and the Lawrence family, who were large investors here. Storrow won but not without dissension.

The year 1997 marks the 150th anniversary of Lawrence's incorporation as a town. This book, though not dealing specifically with the city in the mid-nineteenth century, nonetheless celebrates the people of Lawrence, covering the years 1847–1960. It is intended as a sequel to the first volume, Images of America: *Lawrence, Massachusetts* (1995).

The success of the first book determined that a second volume should follow. Immigrant City Archives (ICA), the historical society of Lawrence, provided many of the images and research materials used in both books. The public too was solicited for photographs.

As chief of research for ICA, I receive inquiries daily from around the country and abroad for information concerning Lawrence's past and the people who lived here. Questions concerning genealogy have tripled over the past few years. Many Europeans are now actively searching out their ancestors who emigrated to Lawrence. Scholarly interest in the city's history is increasing. It is hoped that this sequel will provide readers with an enhanced appreciation of this remarkable community.

Ken Skulski

"Nothing is more responsible for the good old days than a bad memory."

—Robert Benchley

One

On Broadway: North

Broadway was originally called Turnpike Street, a name derived from the Londonderry Turnpike of which it was once a part. The name was not officially changed until 1868. Combining the length of its north and south sides, Broadway is the longest street in the city.

The first physician, school, police station, tailor, barber, boarding house, grocer, attorney, tavern, blacksmith, dentist, saddlemaker, post office, savings bank, and temperance group all began business on Broadway.

Though intended primarily for commercial use, Broadway—especially above Lowell Street—remained a largely residential area until after the Civil War. Construction of the Arlington Mills also hastened growth.

The Broadway Theater is shown above during the opening week of *Gone with the Wind* in 1939. This motion picture theater was situated diagonally across the street from the Victoria Theater, which opened in 1910.

This panoramic view shows the junction of Broadway and Essex Streets—Lawrence's premier intersection—as it looked in 1910. At left is the post office building, barely five years old when this photograph was shot. Crossing Broadway, the Franklin Hotel with its mansard roof is at right, appearing as though it were attached to the group of ten-footers on the corner of Essex Street. To the right of the trolley cars, the massive Brechin Block stands. In this same year, just a little further up Broadway, the first of Theater Row's movie houses opened. Despite the excitement and draw of this theater district over the years, Broadway never acquired either the allure or sophistication of Essex Street, nor was it ever as much of a commercial success.

In 1845 the first boarding house was built on Broadway between Valley and Common Streets for Timothy Osgood and his wife. A scarcity of housing meant that up to two hundred masons, stonecutters, and laborers might sleep here a night. A year later the first post office opened on the opposite side of the street not far from the building seen in this 1910 photograph. At the southeast corner of Broadway and Essex Street, where the Brechin Block appears here, the first engine house was constructed for the Essex Company's hand tub. Two of Lawrence's original hotels, the Coburn House (seen here as the Franklin Hotel) and the Merrimack House (on the corner of Tremont Street) were built on Broadway in 1847.

Looking northerly up Broadway from the intersection of Common Street, this c. 1906 postcard view shows the area before any theaters were built. At left is the Post Office Square Hotel, once among the city's largest. Virtually all of the structures visible at right have been destroyed.

At Christmastime the bar in the Post Office Square Hotel usually employed three bartenders. That's Stephen Orroth standing beneath the clock c. 1914. The hotel, a survivor of Lawrence's early days, has undergone numerous alterations and name changes. In the late 1940s three of its five stories were removed. A White Tower hamburger stand operated here through World War II. From 1931 to 1985 the Pearl family sold popcorn and nuts here. A market and travel agency currently occupy the building.

Lebanese immigrants began the U-Save Market at 252 Broadway in 1921 when the Yameen family, which now owns Butcher Boy Meat Markets, opened their store at this address. Today the Racicot Funeral Home conducts business here. Although the area was largely a French-Canadian neighborhood when this *c.* 1923 photograph was taken, many other nationalities lived and ran stores at this Route 28 crossroads. The Italian Cunio family, whose fruit store awning appears at right, long occupied the northeast corner of Broadway and Haverhill Streets.

Frank L. Kidd started as a carpenter and painter in the late nineteenth century while living on Cross Street. By 1900 the Lawrence native owned this popular hardware store at 198 Broadway, eventually moving to 240 Broadway. Due to ill health, Kidd returned to painting as a contractor until his death in 1942. At right in this *c.* 1914 photograph is Frank Stevens, a painter (and Kidd's brother-in-law). By World War II Kidd's was one of five hardware stores on Broadway.

Although cigar store Indians were once a fairly common feature at local tobacconists, this multicolored rarity—a female—is remembered by more than one generation of city shoppers. Standing next to her in this late 1930s photograph is David Haynes, a Canadian of English ancestry, whose smoke shop was situated at 194 Broadway for some three score years. Haynes, himself a snuff user, exhibited this antique at the store until his death in 1939. This business, and the Indian, were later sold to Nemerow Bros., located a few doors up the street in the Eagles Hall building at 204 Broadway.

D.F. Robinson, a card clothing manufacturer from Fremont, New Hampshire, built this still impressive brick factory at 170 Broadway on the corner of Lowell Street in 1882. It is one of the very few factories ever constructed on Broadway and has seen many modifications. In this c. 1910 view, a popular apothecary shares frontage with the Merrimac Supply Company, which also sold gas fittings. From 1919 to 1969 this was home to the Lawrence Lodge of Elks #65 BPOE.

Lawrencians were introduced to the 5¢ hot dog on this block when George Chatis, a Greek immigrant, opened George's Tasty Lunch in 1922 at 217 Broadway (seen at right in this *c.* 1960 photograph, between the two cars). Dinners ran about 20¢ each and the proximity to Theater Row made George's a midnight magnet. Chatis was selling his franks for less than two bits when urban renewal took the building in 1969. A strip mall now occupies the east side of Broadway from Bradford to Concord Streets.

Beginning in 1934, the Paradise Dine & Dance at 198 Broadway, with its dark, reflective, art-deco facade, quickly became a city landmark. During World War II, Chef Leo Nadeau's baked lobster pie was the preferred house specialty. Besides featuring floor shows at 9 and 11 pm, the Paradise also drew crowds to hear a young Chestnut Street musician and WLAW radio star named Guy Borrelli play piano. Lasting barely through the 1940s, the Paradise was eventually consumed by fire.

Before the Lawrence Post Office was erected on the west side of Broadway in 1905, its site was occupied by a park often called Depot Square Park. In this southerly view photographed just prior to 1905, the park can be seen almost at center surrounded by trees. A McDonald's restaurant currently operates here. Taken from the northeast corner of Common Street, this shot also reveals the Boston & Maine North Station Depot and tower, long since gone.

The daily transport of freight around Lawrence was usually accomplished with horse-drawn vehicles well into the twentieth century. Job wagons with their teamsters could regularly be found either at the busy corners of Broadway and Essex or Broadway and Common Streets. As this c. 1907 photograph shows, motorized vehicles were steadily increasing in commercial use. Here Thomas Firth sits behind the wheel of an IHC delivery truck as a driver for Jackson's Parcel Express, which then maintained offices at both 291 and 237 1/2 Broadway.

16

The construction of most remaining Arlington Mill buildings was completed between 1880 and 1925. This gate, which once stood on the west side of Broadway facing Park Street, was among those built in the latter part of the nineteenth century and was attached to the clock tower.

Through the fall and winter of 1893–94 the poet Robert Frost was employed by this mill, where nearly a thousand arc lights burned, as a light trimmer. His poems, "A Lone Striker" and "The Mill City," recall this time.

Composer Leonard Bernstein's mother, Jennie Resnick, worked as a weaver's helper in these mills while still a teenager before and after the 1912 strike.

As in the work stoppage of 1912, the textile strike of 1919 was often violent, with accusations of radicalism made against its leaders. Lasting fifteen weeks, it ended when strikers accepted a forty-eight-hour work week without a cut in pay. Here, on the southeast corner of Broadway and Park Streets, mounted police control a crowd across from the Arlington Mill Park Street gate (seen above). The caption on this postcard reads "Savage Cossacks attacking strikers, Lawrence, Feb. 1919."

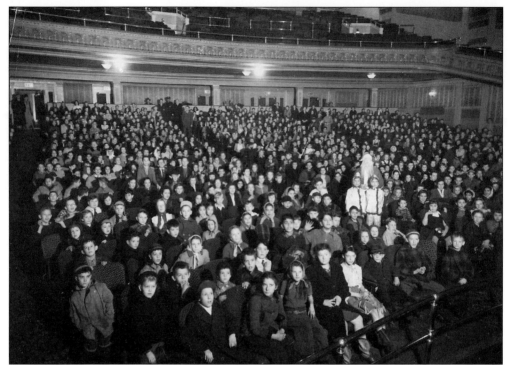

Designed by local architect James E. Allen for Michael Morris and his partner, Louis B. Mayer of Haverhill, the 1,700-seat Broadway Theater began its sixty-eight years of life in the fall of 1910 offering silent movies and vaudeville. Costing over $100,000 to build, it was probably the first theater in Lawrence constructed expressly for motion pictures. This 1947 photograph of a union-sponsored Christmas party for city children provides a rare, unobstructed view taken from stage left.

For generations, a favorite recollection of Broadway surely included Theater Row, pictured here in the 1920s. The popular district consisted of four movie houses on the west side of Broadway above Common Street: the Broadway Theater was the first to open in 1910, followed by the Strand in 1917, and the Palace and Modern in 1921. The popularity of inner-city theaters declined in the early 1960s. By the late 1970s Theater Row was demolished, except for the Strand.

Incorporated in 1894 by and for employees of the Arlington Mills, the Arlington Co-operative Association's central store was located at 479–481 Broadway in a brick building at the northeast corner of Holly Street. This later became the Star Theater. Members owned shares and bought groceries, shoes, clothing, wood, coal, and household items in this emporium or at one of its branches. There was pride in membership, as is displayed in this convoy of members entering the 1903 Semi-Centennial Parade.

Charles Starbard became the first manager of the Star Family Theater when it opened around 1913. Its name may have come from his; no one knows for sure. A cooperative store had been transformed into a motion picture theater, the only one in the Arlington district. Frank Boscketti, an owner, added the trademark brick facade. Close to the Spicket River, the Star was disinfected daily. Movies changed two or three times a week. It was sold and leveled in 1966.

Dr. Sylvester Melven, born in 1834, sits outside 332 Broadway on the corner of Florence Street c. 1875. Besides being a home recently built for his family—perhaps the most substantial brick house ever constructed on Broadway—this dwelling was also designed as a factory and sales office where he developed his own brands of hair restorer. This New Hampshire native worked in the Lowell mills before learning dentistry. Following the Civil War, he and his bride settled here, where Melven continued as a respected patent medicine manufacturer until his death. The house still stands.

Max Nevins and Max Warshaw, two young Jewish businessmen, began the Nevins Auto Company in 1919. By 1925, when this photograph was taken, their auto showroom (displaying Peerless, Velie, and Dart motor cars) was situated at 400 Broadway, seen at the bottom left in this view looking north from Cross Street. Many Jews had originally settled in the Arlington district. Both Joel Daniels, who sold stoves, and Nathan Pearl, an umbrella salesman, were also operating businesses then on this west side block.

20

Saloonkeeper Patrick Dempsey owned this brick block at 103–109 Broadway in the early 1870s. He may have been the original proprietor. For virtually all of its existence (urban renewal claimed the building in the late 1960s), some type of liquor establishment flourished in this building on the southeast corner of Valley Street. In this *c.* 1960 photograph, Eugene McCarthy's Manhattan Lounge appears at right, fondly remembered as a favorite St. Patrick's Day rendezvous for politicians and Irishmen (some were both!) in the 1950s.

Now extinct, butcher shops like the one pictured in this *c.* 1910 photograph were once a common presence on Broadway. Confectioners, horse shoers, bowling alleys, shoeshine parlors, sausagemakers, coffin warehouses, paper hangers, and greenhouses all had a place on this most democratic of city streets. Hardly a profession, trade, service, article of merchandise, or ethnic group could be found that did not at some time have a representative on Broadway. Could one say the same for another Lawrence thoroughfare?

Opening on Labor Day in 1959, Jesser's had recently purchased these two Joubert-family owned eateries at 205–207 Broadway. Abraham Rahhal from Gareva, Lebanon, actually began what later became known as Jesser's Restaurant by operating a variety of predecessors in Lawrence beginning in the 1920s. His death in 1948 left son Wallace and daughter Nazar Rahhal Jesser to run the business.

A fresh kibbee sandwich here in the late '50s included French fries and a salad and sold for only 75¢. The restaurant closed in 1972.

Everyday life on Broadway during the 1880s is dramatically revealed in this candid photograph taken around the burgeoning Arlington Mills, which are being remodeled. These mills were the first in the U.S. to successfully manufacture mohairs, black alpacas, and brilliantines. Traffic is heavy. The maximum speed limit on Lawrence streets at the time was 6 mph. By 1918, the Arlington Mills covered 49 acres off Broadway and employed almost 7,000 workers producing worsted wear, worsted yarns, and tops.

Pianos, safes, boilers, and machinery were most often moved out of windows or around and beyond the city by specialists in heavy trucking. By 1912, foremost among those in this business was Henry C. Tetreau, whose office and employment bureau were located on the southwest corner of Broadway and Essex Streets. Though much in demand, such work was hard with a high turnover of help. Tetreau also maintained a stable at 109 Water Street.

St. John's Episcopal Church was not officially organized until May of 1886, though services were conducted in the Essex Engine House on Morton Street since before the Civil War. Around 1870 this parish moved to Bradford Street. It stayed there until 1903, when Boston architect Charles Cummings designed the structure above. Built just beyond Florence Street at 342 Broadway, this church is no longer extant though the parish survives as part of St. Andrew's in Methuen.

Following a disastrous fire at Brechin Block in 1924, businesses located here began rebuilding. In this c. 1928 photograph looking at the southeast corner of Broadway and Essex Street, the building in the center is the portion of Brechin Block that survived the fire. It was renovated, becoming the Broadway Savings Bank. Situated next to it at left is Treat Hardware's Essex Street store. Treat's Broadway store appears behind the bank. Sandwiched between the two is Dempsey's little lunch cart.

The Merrimack Valley Horse Railroad began operating on Broadway in the winter of 1867. Horse-drawn vehicles then had only straw for passengers to plug up drafts. In 1891, when electric trolleys were introduced, riders finally had a central heating stove in each car. Above, citizens cross Essex Street c. 1907 from the Needham Hotel transfer station near Broadway. In-town travel cost about 5¢. A trip to Haverhill took around forty-five minutes and cost 15¢.

In the late 1880s, Spruce Street resident Charles E. Merrill went from being a carpenter to a grocer. By 1910, eight years before his death, he successfully employed three assistants at this 2,800-square-foot establishment on the bustling northwest corner of Manchester Street.

While most shopping in the late nineteenth century was done daily, on credit, and by women, fixed prices were uncommon. Here, Merrill boldly publishes his on this amusing, eye-grabbing handout. Unfortunately, this enterprise did not long survive his passing. The building itself lasted only into the 1920s.

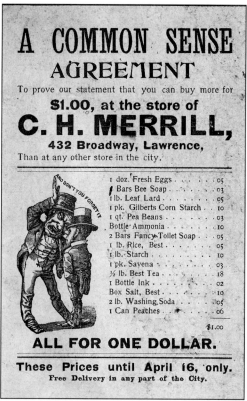

A COMMON SENSE
AGREEMENT
To prove our statement that you can buy more for
$1.00, at the store of
C. H. MERRILL,
432 Broadway, Lawrence,
Than at any other store in the city.

1 doz. Fresh Eggs	05
1 Bars Bee Soap	03
1 lb. Leaf Lard	05
1 pk. Gilberts Corn Starch	10
1 qt. Pea Beans	03
Bottle Ammonia	10
2 Bars Fancy Toilet Soap	05
1 lb. Rice, Best	05
1 lb. Starch	10
1 pk. Sayena	03
½ lb. Best Tea	18
1 Bottle Ink	02
Box Salt, Best	10
2 lb. Washing Soda	05
1 Can Peaches	06
	$1.00

ALL FOR ONE DOLLAR.

These Prices until April 16, only.
Free Delivery in any part of the City.

Looking east from the J.A. Leone & Sons parking lot, the Flamingo Lounge at 301 Broadway is nearly at center in this c. 1956 photograph. With its trademark flamingo bird sign extending above the roof, this popular nightclub (which succeeded John Callahan's Cal-C-Mo Café) survived only to burn ten years later in a $250,000 fire. Like the Silver Slipper, Larry's The Wonder Bar, and Bea's, it was an integral part of Broadway nightlife through the 1950s.

Brocatelle, hair cloth parlor sets, chamber pots, bench wringers, and oil cloth were among the fashionable items selling at James Tonge's Arlington District Furniture Store in the 1890s. Tonge, a Pacific Mill operative who entered the mercantile trade in the 1880s, stands at the doorway to his 440 Broadway concern. Besides new and used furniture, ice boxes and cast-iron stoves were a specialty.

Foley, Donovan & Chadwick succeeded Tonge in 1919. By the late 1920s this building ceased to exist. Today, the property is but one portion of a parking lot.

Taken June 4, 1896, this cyanotype of Broadway's east side near the intersection of Canal Street shows the construction of the Pacific Mill #6 Storehouse. Built as a repository for finished goods, this storehouse was once connected by an overhead iron bridge to Storehouse #1 (now called the Lorenzo Building) on the northwest corner of Franklin and Canal Streets. By 1924, these were but two of over twenty-seven structures in Lawrence maintained by this textile-manufacturing giant.

Two
On Broadway: South

Broadway was a prime access road used during construction of the Great Stone Dam. Approximately 1.67 miles of the street is in South Lawrence where it becomes South Broadway. By 1875 little existed on South Broadway above Andover Street. Most dwellings and commercial development then were situated on the west side of South Broadway. Irish and French-Canadians became the principal residents of South Lawrence following the Civil War. Even today, their houses of worship are the only Roman Catholic churches on the entire length of Broadway. St. Patrick's steeple dominates the street in this c. 1906 postcard view looking up South Broadway from the intersection of Merrimack Street.

This view of the approach to South Broadway from North Lawrence across the Falls Bridge was taken c. 1910 from the roof of the USWOCO Mills. In 1881, the iron bridge seen here was erected, replacing wooden structures which had spanned this Merrimack River crossing since 1793. From the construction of the Great Stone Dam (1845–1848), at left, until the opening of Interstate 495, this was the most traveled area in the city. Lafayette became the first celebrity to pass here in 1825.

Looking from atop the City Flour Mill near South Broadway c. 1890 we see the South Canal, which was constructed beginning in 1866. To the left of the canal is the Monroe Felt & Paper Company, which became the Merrimack Paper Company in 1881. Merrimack Street is at right. This was one of the most heavily trafficked parts of nineteenth-century South Broadway. Though much of it looks the same today, the Moseley truss bridge and the City Flour Mill are gone.

The first firehouse in South Lawrence was a small wooden one erected in 1850 on the northwest corner of South Broadway and Crosby Streets. It cost about $2,000 to build and stood until after the Civil War, when this brick building was completed. Prior to 1854, men pulled apparatus to fires in Lawrence. When horses, steam fire wagons, and larger equipment were introduced, more space was needed. Those great towers were not built for bells or as a lookout, but for drying hoses. A still larger, more modern brick firehouse replaced this one in the 1930s.

According to the Reverend George Packard, an early school superintendent, the Saunders Schoolhouse began life in 1850 on the corner of Winthrop Avenue and Andover Street. By 1860 the structure was moved here to the northwest corner of South Broadway and Chester Street (Bowdoin Street had not yet been laid out). Named for Daniel Saunders, considered by some to be the founder of Lawrence, this two-story, six-room wooden schoolhouse was situated across the street from Mr. Saunders' home. The school suffered numerous fires and was often renovated. The present brick building replaced this one in 1931.

Junior firemen line up in front of Conlin & Ryan's Funeral Parlor at 59 South Broadway near Engine 3 in 1903. As part of an official celebration of the city's 50th anniversary, each youngster wears a dress uniform for a parade. Fire horns, held by some boys, were used by firefighters to holler commands during a conflagration. The small hand pumper at center is a real piece of apparatus that survives today in the care of Immigrant City Archives.

John Daly, an Irish immigrant and grocer, built this brick block at 87–91 South Broadway around 1889. Daly maintained one of the city's busiest meat markets here while his son ran a saloon next door. The upper floors were for tenants. Neighborhood children were often hired by the Daly family to put up potatoes in peck bags. Their day's pay was 5¢ plus all the pickles and apples they could eat. Josiah Crosby, for whom Crosby Street is named, opened Lawrence's first grocery in 1845 on South Broadway (then Turnpike Street).

Prior to the Flood of 1936, the Great Cyclone of July 26, 1890, was the worst natural disaster to strike South Lawrence. Although only a small portion of South Broadway was affected, St. Patrick's Church was damaged. This view taken from the northeast corner of the building on Salem Street shows where a large stained-glass window and the east side of the vestry's pitch roof were destroyed. Six of those killed by this tornado were parishioners of St. Patrick's.

St. Patrick's is the oldest Catholic parish in South Lawrence. Begun as a mission church of Immaculate Conception in North Lawrence, a small wooden chapel was built on a plot at the southeast corner of South Broadway and Salem Streets purchased in 1868. Growing numbers of Irish in South Lawrence required a larger structure. The current church was completed in 1894. May processions, like this one on South Broadway in the 1950s, began at St. Patrick's in the 1920s.

Remembered fondly as "Paytrick's" (pronounced with a Gaelic flourish), this drugstore at 122 South Broadway was begun by Frank Emerson, a city druggist. Each of the south side's three apothecaries was then situated on South Broadway. In 1910 John W. Patrick, a North Andover native and eighteen-year employee of Emerson's, took over the operation, which had been renamed Emerson and Patrick in 1906. Besides proprietary medicines, Patrick's became known for its advertised temperance beverages and soda fountain. Arthur and Mary McCormick, who were both pharmacists as well as being siblings, ran the business for its last fifty years of life.

Herman Bruckmann arrived in Lawrence around 1868. An immigrant from Saxony, he labored in the mills before establishing this grain and feed store in 1886 at 158 South Broadway. Besides selling grain, hay, straw, poultry supplies, and fertilizers, Bruckmann specialized in rye flour. Though not the first or the only enterprise offering grain and feed, it was probably the most diverse. By 1968 the store moved across the street to 179 South Broadway. It remains one of the oldest continuously run businesses in all of Lawrence.

Congregationalists were the first Protestant denomination to begin worship in South Lawrence. Starting in 1852 on Andover Street, two laymen formed a Sunday school. Eventually, services were held in the firehouse on South Broadway and later at the B&M Railroad Station off Andover Street. A separate chapel was built and dedicated on South Broadway in 1859. In the 1860s it was replaced by this wooden structure in which, in 1868, the South Congregational Church was organized.

By the end of the nineteenth century a flourishing parish made obvious the need for a larger building. During the pastorate of the Reverend Clark Carter, a Sabbath school for arriving Chinese was established. In 1859 work began on the edifice seen here. Erected on the same site, it replaced the little chapel the following year. On the evening of April 23, 1939, a fierce blaze destroyed this structure. The present building was dedicated in 1940.

Looking from the northeast corner of South Broadway down Inman Street we see the headquarters of the D.W. Pingree Company, a lumber dealer specializing in clapboards, laths, cloth boards, and shingles. Pingree also became a principal manufacturer of wooden boxes. Incorporated in 1893, by 1910, when this photograph appeared, the company covered some 9 acres and employed nearly two hundred men. Lasting into the early 1970s, Pingree's was finally consumed by a fast-moving fire.

The crossroads at Andover Street was, even before the Revolutionary War, an important Andover settlement. The Shawsheen and Essex Taverns were once located there. On the southeast corner, shown above, Elihu Webster ran a hotel prior to the Civil War. Called Webster House, it changed hands numerous times. In the 1920s, Smith Chevrolet sold cars here. By the 1930s, when this postcard was published, Texaco had opened a service station that thrived well into the 1960s.

Begun in 1900 as a mission church of St. Anne's in North Lawrence, the Sacred Heart Mission had the original intent of reaching out to French-Canadian Catholics settling in the rapidly growing area of South Lawrence. French-Canadians constituted the largest group of foreign-born residents in the city. A chapel school, the tall building seen above, was begun that same year on Hawley Street. In 1916 a separate chapel was built on South Broadway, seen here with the large cross.

By 1930 much construction had already been carried out by this now French National Parish. Another larger church was needed for a still blossoming congregation. That year Louis C. Cyr, contractor and mason, was hired to build this new stone church, replacing the brick chapel on South Broadway. Joseph Morrissette was the architect. Work on Sacred Heart Church was completed in November of 1936. Louise Haffner Fournier was the first bride married within.

This *c.* 1955 aerial view taken from above Mt. Vernon Street looking east affords a spectacular view of South Lawrence and the downtown area. South Broadway appears at the bottom left of the picture. Sacred Heart Church is the long structure with the tall steeple. Directly across South Broadway is Nassar Ford. The extensive B&M rail yard behind the Monomac Mills remains. Beyond, South Union Street heads past both the Ayer and Wood Mills into downtown Lawrence. To the left of these mill buildings is the Central Bridge. The Merrimack River winds toward Haverhill at the far right.

Three
Ways We Work

A moment with twenty-six-year-old South Lawrence shoemaker John Hickey in his Border Street workshop was captured on a glass-plate negative *c.* 1897. Carefully posed for this difficult exposure, Hickey was actually employed by the Alfred Kimball Shoe Company on Blanchard Street, where he became a foreman in subsequent years.

Although much attention in the past has been focused on work in the textile industry (Lawrence was the woolen worsted capital of the world by World War I), scores of occupations here have been neglected pictorially. This chapter offers a glimpse into some of the better- and lesser-known jobs, careers, and businesses that flourished in the city, as well as the people who performed and owned them.

Philip Fisichelli, posing outside his barbershop at 75 Union Street *c*. 1936, was born into poverty in Sicily in 1899. While still a boy he emigrated to the U.S. with his older brother Joe. Employed briefly as an operative in the Wood Mill, Phil quickly decided that mill work was not for him. After attending a Boston barber college, he opened this shop, which he ran with his wife (see below). In business for some forty years, Phil was never far from his Sicilian roots. At the family home on East Haverhill Street, he raised goats for milk.

Rose Fisichelli prepares for another client in her beauty salon, located in the rear of her husband's tonsorial chambers (see above) on Union Street, *c*. 1928. An immigrant herself, she and Phil were married at Holy Rosary Church on September 24, 1922, by Father Milanese. Mrs. Fisichelli was the first beautician in the city to administer a Frederic Permanent Wave (given by the electrical contraption dangling at left beside the fern). In 1941 she opened the Peacock Beauty Parlor on the first floor of her 137 East Haverhill Street home.

The Engine 6 firehouse was built in 1896 on Howard Street, where it has stood for over a century. Prior to its construction, the closest fire station to Prospect Hill was Steamer #2 on Garden Street. Here in the early 1950s are the men of Engine 6. From left to right are Bernard Sullivan, William Hey, Robert Stoney, Dan Lorden, John J. Ford, Thomas Troy, Thomas Mulvey, James Garvey, Walter Shea, Ernest Mills, Lieutenant Charles Eichner, and Captain William Manning.

Two Canadian entrepreneurs, Edouard Courtemache (right) and Charles Bernardin (left), began the Canadian Pacific Tea Company here in 1887. Seen outside their 31 Franklin Street store c. 1890, they specialized in tea, coffee, butter, and baking powders while also selling silverware, crockery, lamps, and tinware—with premiums! A growing Franco-American population constituted much of their trade. Each man eventually went his own way, with Courtemache becoming a Lowell Street grocer and Bernardin establishing a long-running butter and egg business on Tower Hill.

Milkmen, ice men, and bakers were daily drivers over the morning streets. H.P. Hood & Sons began delivering milk here before the turn of the century. By 1911 they were supplying city residents daily with some 3,500 quarts from Vermont farms as well as others in southern New Hampshire. Nearly 150 local farms also produced milk then. Much came from Maine. Here a Hood wagon in Lawrence plows through the Flood of 1936.

The H.P. Hood & Sons 425 Market Street workforce poses for this 1936 photograph. Beginning at the top, from left to right, are Jackson, Page, Thompson, Bosse, Mansur, White, McDonald, Waldie, Callahan, Hutchings, Locke, Benewicz, unknown, Hart, McPharland, Parker, Crockett, Ricker, unknown, unknown, Beauchesne, unknown, Weinhold, Murray, Sullivan, Flanders, Colley, unknown, unknown, Green, Ward, unknown, LeClerc, Daigle, Gallant, Dufresne, unknown, unknown, Kelley, Cookson, Page, Whiteside, Hart, Willis, Brannigan, Kimball (manager), McDonald, and Russell.

Oak Street's Bill Ahern, at left, was a patrolman only a short time when this *c.* 1910 photograph was taken at the corner of Broadway and Lowell Street. Ahern, who served for forty years, joined the department when the force was composed largely of men of Irish descent. Originally a plumber, young Bill's favorite beat was Broadway near the theaters. While in pursuit of a suspect, Bill would repeatedly strike his billy club hard on the pavement to alert other patrolmen.

Sitting atop this street sprinkler *c.* 1920 is Cornelius Casey who, as a young man, emigrated from County Cork, Ireland. A street department foreman for over twenty-five years, Casey was also in partnership with his brother Stephen at a coal and wood enterprise on Hampshire Street.

Watering carts were used extensively to keep dirt from blowing everywhere. Prior to 1892 this work was performed by private contractors. These two steeds have just pulled up to a city water trough.

Basket-making in Lawrence was practiced by only a few artisans. James Carney began his business in 1875 at this factory believed to have been on Exchange Street near the Spicket River. Handmade baskets of white oak were much in demand. Oak was preferred for its strength and durability. Carney's baskets were sold to textile mills, paper mills, bobbin shops, and rubber factories. However, he moved often. By the late 1880s Dracut was his home and new business address.

The service staff of the J.W. Robinson Company poses in the rear of 455 Common Street *c.* 1948. Robinson became a Dodge dealer in 1916, ceasing operations in 1956. From left to right are as follows: (front row) Drelick, Dudley, Gartside, Kiernan, Hemmerling, Pettoruto, Huston, Frank, Holland, DeFeo, and Ouellette; (back row) Brown, unknown, Landers, three Dodge salesmen, Chabot, Hill, Dudley, McAuliffe, Brainerd, Fone, Quintal, Ouellette, Tennant, and Veit. In the doorway is L. Kress.

The junk man cometh and taketh away the detritus of our times. Here on Tyler Street in South Lawrence, a junk man's wagon is being loaded *c.* 1900. Most junk dealers in Lawrence at the turn of the century were of Jewish, German, or Irish ancestry. Among the largest of these was Gutterson & Gould, located at 508 Common Street. Rags, paper stock, scrap iron, and metals were especially desirable. Note the unusual location of the bulkhead at the front of this house.

In the late 1920s, grape nut pudding was a favorite dessert in John Curtin's restaurant, the French Cafe, at 47 Franklin Street. The restaurant, which had thirteen stools and ten tables, was where fifteen-year-old Eva Pellerin, at right, was usually busy serving Pacific Mill employees luncheon specials like the vegetable boiled plate that sold for 35¢, including coffee and dessert. Eva, an orphaned Canadian immigrant, earned about $8 a week and worked Sundays. Her unidentified co-worker was a bit older and probably earned more.

Recycling is not new. Jim McGovern, posing outside his farm on North Street in West Andover *c.* 1912, ran a hugely successful three-story rendering plant with one boiler. Dead animals were collected daily off Lawrence streets and brought to be "rendered," after which the end products—hides, tallow, fertilizer—were sold. McGovern was often referred to as "the horse undertaker." He was fond of saying, "No automobile will ever take the place of a horse." He died in the 1920s.

Cigar-making in Lawrence actually dates back to pre-Civil War times when one-man shops began operating at various downtown locations. Stephen F. McDonnell (that's probably him puffing away) was a city native who began manufacturing cigars around the turn of the century. He developed his "1492" 5¢ cigar, made here in a factory at 252 Lowell Street (home to Watts Regulator). By 1910 he employed fifteen people to process the choice Havana tobacco, producing 600,000 cigars annually.

Like many Italians who began emigrating to Lawrence prior to World War I, Michele Manzi, first at left, was an enterprising soul willing to fully explore his opportunities. By turns a laborer, bottler, restaurateur, bartender, proprietor of a billiards parlor, and a grocer, Manzi finally settled on the real estate business. Above at 217–219 Elm Street he's seen in the 1920s with, from left to right, an unidentified businessman and associates Ed Mosca and Antonio Manzi.

By 1895 most of the city's female textile workers earned less than $7 a week. Although women usually outnumbered men in the mills by as much as three to one, they earned only half the pay. Mary Driscoll, standing taller than her co-workers in front of spinning frames at the Pacific Mill, pursued an education. Unlike most female operatives, she graduated from high school and a commercial college, leaving mill work for office work and a career.

Griffin's, Shine's, McQuillan's, and O'Brien's were the major markets on Lawrence Street owned by Irish-Americans in the 1920s. Jim O'Brien, seen behind the counter, and his younger brother William ran this business at the corner of Park Street. O'Brien's had two front entrances, one on Park and one on Lawrence Street, where pickle, flour, and apple barrels seemed positioned to greet you. Through the Depression, O'Brien's carried customers on credit—long credit. Note the dapper salesman with his sample bag.

The Kimball Bros. Shoe Company manufactured men's and boys' footwear sold all over the U.S., Cuba, and the Philippines with contracts in the Sandwich Islands by 1900. Employing over five hundred, the firm produced around two thousand pairs of shoes daily at their Blanchard Street factory, seen here c. 1895. Women workers might average only $5–$6 a week. Shoemaking represented a relatively small portion of industrial production in Lawrence until the mid-twentieth century.

Twenty-one years before there was a New England Typographical Union, Lawrence printers organized in September of 1889. By 1896 they declared themselves to be the first union in New England to work an eight-hour day. In 1910, when the New England union finally succeeded, Lawrence was chosen to host its first convention. Seen in this c. 1920 photograph is the Eagle Tribune composing room. Lorenzo Fecteau, a union member for seventy years, stands second from the left.

The Murray Bros. Company, wholesale grocers, thrived at 617 Common Street close to Broadway near the B&M rail yard. Founded in 1879, the company advertised itself as the sole agent for the Moxie Nerve Food Company and also offered retailers the best in staple and fancy groceries and provisions. Like most wholesalers, they maintained traveling sales representatives and a fleet of delivery wagons similar to the one pictured here c. 1906. Because refrigeration was limited then, multiple deliveries were not uncommon.

The Lithuanian National Corporation Bakery was founded on Holly Street by both Roman and Lithuanian National Catholics in the 1920s. Baking from nine hundred to one thousand loaves a day, their ovens were famous for light and dark rye and raisin breads as well as bagels. These were usually delivered to largely Lithuanian neighborhoods in the Merrimack Valley and southern New Hampshire. The business thrived until the 1960s. The driver in this *c.* 1928 photograph is unidentified.

Ed McCabe arrived from Sherbrooke, Canada, to work on the construction of the Great Stone Dam. From blacksmith to boilermaker, he manufactured dye kettles, tanks, and steam engines for over forty years at his factory on Water Street. The business was continued by the McCabe family into the 1980s. Here in the basement of St. Anne's School, *c.* 1914, a McCabe boiler is being cleaned by the Alfred Bergeron Company, master plumbers, whose office was located around the corner on West Street.

These two Sicilian immigrants are most often credited with introducing pizza into the Lawrence area. Lucia and Salvatore Coco arrived here before World War I, but it was in the early 1940s that Mr. Coco, a baker, thought Lawrencians might enjoy this Italian delicacy. At this storefront on the corner of Middle and Garden Streets he christened his new enterprise, Napoli Pizza, where each slice then sold for 10¢ and two bits bought you a big meat pie. Both the building and Middle Street are no longer extant.

"A teacher is better than two books," goes the German proverb. Of the first six teachers hired by the Town of Lawrence in 1847, five were women. But men were often paid more than their female counterparts. Out of 260 elementary teachers in 1913, only 7 were men. All taught in rooms similar to this third-grade classroom at the Hood School on Park Street. However, a male director of music or drawing received twice the salary of an equally qualified female.

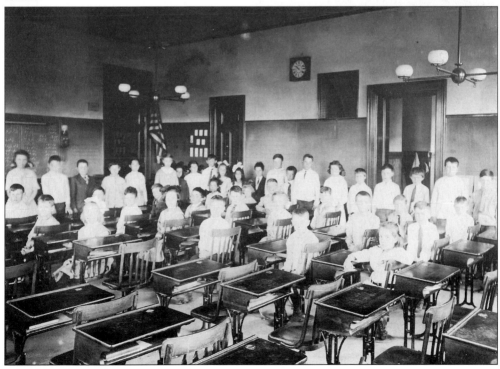

The push-cart patrol was a common feature of the Lawrence Street Department prior to World War I. The carts were usually deployed only on paved streets and often were accompanied by machine sweepers. Twice a year all streets were scraped and cleaned by hand. In 1909 eleven push-cart patrols cleaned four streets—Essex, Broadway, South Broadway, and Common—on a regular basis for $2 a day. Who was deemed most responsible for dirtying the city's streets in 1906? The shopkeepers.

Begun in 1919, the Arlington Mills Band survived after the mills closed in the 1950s. April 16, 1919, was the date of the group's first big event, welcoming returning veterans. Noon concerts outside the mill were often daily happenings. The band was comprised of actual mill workers who were also professional musicians. They played at concerts, parades, May processions, and even the 1940 World's Fair. Their uniforms were black with gold buttons and braid. This *c*. 1920 photograph shows the original bandleader, George Tetley, fifth from the left in the front row.

Mrs. Martin Burns stands in the doorway of her well-stocked dry goods store at 294 Park Street c. 1894. Besides operating the only dry goods store run by a woman in Lawrence then, Mrs. Burns was also a skilled milliner and dressmaker. As was customary for many merchants at that time, she resided directly above her enterprise. Mrs. Burns later opened a shop around the corner on Broadway.

Like many first-generation ethnic businesses in the city, the South Lawrence Flooring Company on Easton Street often hired associates from the old country to work here. Several of the men in this c. 1959 photograph were Canadian émigrés. From left to right are Joe Marisola, Joe Boyd, Joe Bottai, Ron Jean, Frank Houle, Francis Ellis, Jean Rancourt, Ray Guillemette, Jack Smith, unknown, Joe Goings, Leo Gallipeau, Emil Daignault, Henry Houle, Arthur Joncas, and Lucien Joncas (proprietor and founder).

The Cochichewick Ice Company was a local business specializing in lake ice cut from Lake Cochichewick in North Andover. By 1894 the company advertised its product as "pure Spring Water where no sewerage or other, poisonous matters enter." Most Lawrence ice companies harvested their crop principally from the Merrimack River. However, ice famines were not uncommon. Sultry winters necessitated hauling in ice from New Hampshire. This photograph of a delivery wagon on Bruce Street was shot *c*. 1902.

Farris Marad played an important role in the strike of 1912. As a leader of the Lebanese on the strike committee, Marad led a parade one day and was arrested the next when dynamite was discovered at his 294 Oak Street tailor shop. It had been planted by the opposition. This immigrant from Jditha, Lebanon, was also a court reporter and special constable. He poses during Christmastime *c*. 1950 in the SAC Club at 352 Elm Street, which he managed for many years.

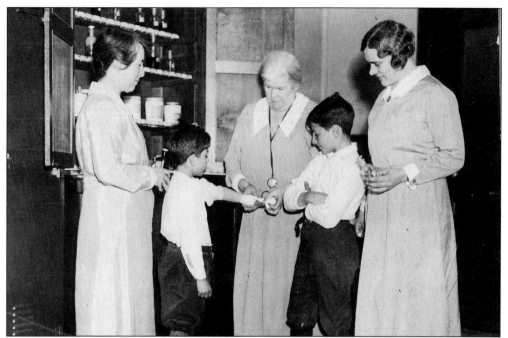

Known affectionately as the "Sister Kenny of Lawrence," Mary T. Murphy, RN (at center) became a public health nurse here in 1912. She devoted her considerable skills to children afflicted with infantile paralysis. "No woman was more quietly esteemed in Lawrence, " recalled one longtime associate. In 1926 Murphy was chosen as director of child welfare for the city. She is shown above in 1936 with nurses Josephine Sullivan and Helen Weigel. She died in 1941.

Essex Company employees are pictured repairing flashboards atop the Great Stone Dam c. 1894. Flashboards are used to increase the depth of water on a dam. This procedure is still done in much the same way today. Note that this repair scow was designed with an outhouse attachment. Besides selling land and leasing water powers, the Essex Company has been responsible for maintaining the dam and canals since their construction.

Newsboys were also part of the daily hustle. Here in 1932 a group poses in front of the Eagle Tribune building on Essex Street. Having won a circulation contest, they would soon leave for a trip to New York City. From left to right are as follows: (front row) W. Noon; (middle row) I. Sbona, L. Marcoux, G. McNiece, G. Wurzbacher, W. Rogoz, J. Haggerty, and M. Worcester; (back row) P. Brailsford (circulation manager), C. Der Garabedian, W. Brown, G. Ruffen, and S. Das.

Taken following the conclusion of the 1912 textile strike, this rare view of the boiler house in the Pacific Mills Power Station off Essex Street showcases a new coal conveyor, above. It was in these buildings that the massive Upper Pacific Mills generated power to its buildings in North Lawrence. Besides being extremely dirty, workers here were often exposed to many of the same health hazards faced daily by coal miners in the South. Built in 1907, these structures still exist.

Isaac Edward Allston arrived in Lawrence from North Carolina in the latter part of the nineteenth century. Seen here about age twenty-five, he was employed for many years at the Franklin Hotel as a porter. A dedicated family man and longtime city resident, his death came in 1937 during the Great Depression. Like most African-Americans in Lawrence at the turn of the century, Mr. Allston was more likely to find work in a service-related occupation, in construction, or on the railroad rather than in manufacturing. Descendants of Isaac and his wife Varneta continue on in Lawrence today.

Prominent in the French-Canadian community of North Lawrence, Victor LeClerc, at left, had been in business for himself for about twenty-four years when this photograph was taken c. 1926. As a respected dealer in wood, coal, and charcoal, Leclerc's 206 Lowell Street office and yard were especially busy early in the morning as deliveries began well before dawn. Fourth from left is longtime delivery man Joe Levesque. Park Hegarty Porsche Audi now takes up a portion of this site.

Lebanese immigrants began settling in Lawrence during the 1890s. Part of the Turkish Empire, they were most often referred to as Syrians. George Ferris, the butcher in white, arrived from Kab Elias, Mount Lebanon, before the First World War, beginning this meat market at 32 White Street in the Plains. So trusted was Ferris that most customers relied implicitly upon his choices in meats over their own. During the Depression the market moved to Swan Street in Methuen.

An unidentified employee of the Lawrence Gas & Electric Company is seen servicing a carbon street light c. 1885. These were used extensively before gas-burning lights were introduced. However, street lamps were not necessarily lit every evening, but rather only on those nights when there was no moon. Police could act as lamplighters, igniting those lights they felt necessary. By the 1880s it was the responsibility of the police to extinguish street lamps by 11 pm.

Lawrence postal workers became part of the National Association of Letter Carriers on April 15, 1891. The organization has survived over a century. Branch 212 members are shown behind the old post office building on Broadway in September of 1952. From left to right are as follows: (front row) Bergeron, Hartnett, Buckley, Bernhardt, Morrison, Nassif, Bohnwagner, Gleason, Pomerleau, Coughlin, and Herdegen; (back row) Minahan, Donahue, White, Hart, Stansfield, Bresnahan, McKenna, Barton, Griffin, Lafleur, McLaughlin, Salach, and Bastian.

Though apparently a proud and satisfied crew when this picture was taken c. 1905, the Stone family did not long continue their variety store here at 210 Water Street on the corner of Caulkin's Court. Within a few years Charles and his wife Annie migrated to West Andover, where he became a farmer off North Street. The Gurdy's Ice Cream advertised in the window was soon to become more widely known and appreciated as the name changed to Jersey Ice Cream.

Work all day and then attend a union meeting at night. Members of the Textile Workers Union of America, Local 227 of Lawrence, sit waiting for a meeting to begin in the winter of 1942. Seated in the front row at bottom right is Ralph Arivella, an organizer at the Wood and Ayer Mills. Arivella was the business agent for the union at their office in the Blakeley Building on Essex Street. A strong trade unionist, he began as a mill worker, rising to prominence in the AFL-CIO.

Shoveling snow, putting up vegetables, sweeping stores, picking fruit, and hawking newspapers were among the better-known, legitimate means for young people to earn extra money in the nineteenth century. A more obscure but no less profitable opportunity lay in delivering lunch pails to mill workers for around 25¢ a week. Hot food and tea were often placed in tin dinner pails similar to those seen depicted here in front of the Pacific Mills. One child might deliver a half-dozen of these daily.

Four
Ways We Relax

By 1920 most ethnic groups had their own clubs and societies: the Portuguese had 2; the British, 2; Jews, 3; Armenians, 5; Lebanese/Syrians, 6; Irish, 8; Polish, 9; French and Franco-Belgian, 14; Lithuanian, 18; Italians, 32; and the Germans, a staggering 47! Besides these there were athletic clubs, glee clubs, shooting clubs, boating clubs, fraternal groups, and literally hundreds of indoor and outdoor sporting events going on year-round. The city contained a dynamic theater district, lecture halls, parks, dance halls, bath houses, pool rooms, delicatessens, oyster houses, speakeasies, restaurants, cafes, and coffee houses, plus the county's largest shopping area. By 1920, fifty-six churches and three synagogues covered the city. All this in an area barely 7 square miles.

Louise Stiritz and Elsie Klunard stand atop the Immigrant City on Prospect Street in Diamond Spring Brewing Company softball uniforms *c.* 1934.

The beaches and the mountains were among the fashionable destinations for turn-of-the-century city residents in the summer, just like today. Lawrence's Arthur Horrock, conductor for the Bay State Street Railway, and Henry Kelley, motorman for the same system, conducted weekly excursions to the Massachusetts North Shore and southern New Hampshire. On this c. 1915 trip, parishioners of the United Congregational Church of Warren Street prepare to visit Marblehead. A trolley ride from Andover Square to Lawrence took about thirty minutes.

Much of life centered around one's church. Most residents lived within walking distance of a house of worship. Participation in church activities was seen as a necessary adjunct to one's public and private life. Feasts, fund-raisers, and services provided solidarity and comfort in shared experience and a belief in God. Here, Pastor Hollenbach of the German Methodist Church oversees an Erntedankfest (Thanksgiving feast) in his Vine Street chapel c. 1922.

Lawrence was devoted to music and the Italians were especially proud of their bands. Among the most stylish was the Royal Club Band, a social club composed of Italian employees of the American Woolen Company. Organized in 1914, they wore black uniforms with trimmings of light blue.

Appearing in this 1920 photograph are, from left to right, as follows: (front row) Frank Grilla, Antonio Grieces, Carlo Pucci, Pietro Lama (director), James Sorbo, Tom Nazzareno, Alfredo Di Angelis, and Ciro Di Vincenzis; (second row) Mike Di Fancesco, Sal Corfi, Filadelfio Faro, Benny Jordano, Nick Cosale, Tony Cestrone, Placido Spitoliera, James Gianni, and Sal Bosco; (third row) Cirino Ferraro, Sabato Di Stefano, Tony Manicini, Gioacachino Angelone, Francesco Giaruso, Phil Di Prima, Tony Artiggiano, Paulo Linares, and Innocenzo Izzo; (back row) Giovanni Gorfi, Tony Grella, Al Jannone, Andrea Di Noto, Dom Schiavone, Emile Pelliccione, James Buonanno, Tony Gorfi, and Jim Grella.

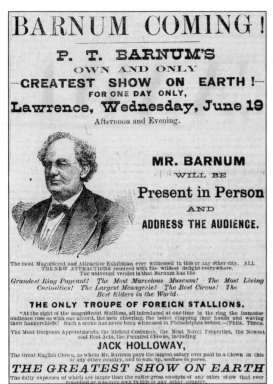

BARNUM COMING!

P. T. BARNUM'S
OWN AND ONLY
—GREATEST SHOW ON EARTH !—
FOR ONE DAY ONLY,
Lawrence, Wednesday, June 19
Afternoon and Evening.

MR. BARNUM
WILL BE

Present in Person
AND

ADDRESS THE AUDIENCE.

The most Magnificent and Attractive Exhibition ever witnessed in this or any other city. ALL THE NEW ATTRACTIONS received with the wildest delight everywhere. The universal verdict is that Barnum has the

Grandest Ring Pageant! The Most Marvelous Museum! The Most Living Curiosities! The Largest Menagerie! The Best Circus! The Best Riders in the World.

THE ONLY TROUPE OF FOREIGN STALLIONS.

"At the sight of the magnificent Stallions, all introduced at one time in the ring the immense audience rose as with one accord, the men cheering, the ladies clapping their hands and waving their handkerchiefs! Such a scene has never been witnessed in Philadelphia before.—(Phila. Times.

The Most Gorgeous Appointments, the Richest Costumes, the Most Novel Properties, the Newest and Best Acts, the Funniest Clowns, including

JACK HOLLOWAY,

The Great English Clown, to whom Mr. Barnum pays the largest salary ever paid to a Clown in this or any other country, and to sum up, *multum in parvo.*

THE GREATEST SHOW ON EARTH

The daily expenses of which are larger than the entire gross receipts of any other show that ever travelled or was ever seen in this or any other country.

Elephants in the Merrimack. Baboons on Broadway. P.T. Barnum himself brought his "greatest show on earth" to the city many times. Within a few hours of his arrival, the south side of Essex Street was transformed into circus grounds. Massive pachyderms were washed in the river. But alas, when the circus arrived so did much less desirable traveling shows like pickpockets, burglars, prostitutes, and con artists. The pickings were ripe. An estimated 12,000 people attended Barnum's Lawrence shows in 1878 according to one newspaper.

Employees of the Kimball Shoe Company invested their free time constructing this monumental entry for the 1903 Semi-Centennial Parade. Posing outside their Blanchard Street factory, they are wearing handmade costumes. Lawrencians loved participating in public events. Holidays offered the best opportunities.

Fourth of July celebrations were especially memorable, with an early morning "horribles" parade followed by sports featuring local athletes, much food, drink, music, and song, and concluding with fireworks and a bonfire.

"Chapeau Coffee Hours" in 1952 were a good way for ladies to help raise money for the YWCA. Women still wore hats to church and most social functions in the '50s. Ruth Wills of Cherry & Webb on Essex Street conducted the event in the Y auditorium. Besides hats made by staff members, furs and accessories were also modeled. Motion picture actress Priscilla Lane (Howard), an Andover resident and Lawrence Y supporter standing first at right, was among the models.

Churches offered gifted amateurs a chance to be heard by captive audiences. Grace Church started its choir, pictured around 1910, in the 1850s when most choirs were exclusively male. Nineteenth-century composer George Whitefield Chadwick launched his distinguished career as an organist for various Lawrence churches. Henry Kemble Oliver, mayor in 1859, was a nationally recognized composer of church music. As a youth, the popular recording star Robert Goulet, a Lawrence native, sang soprano in the choir of St. Anne's Church.

Since 1847, fraternalism flourished in Lawrence. The Masons, Odd Fellows, Elks, Pythians, United Workmen, Hibernians, and Pilgrim Fathers were among the many successful secret organizations with loyalists here.

Seated is Max Naefe, one of eighteen children, who emigrated from Hohlstein-Einstadt, Saxony, around 1880. Max was by trade a loomfixer. Married twice, he lived in a three-decker on Cornish Street. Max was also a dedicated 32nd Degree Mason belonging to both the Bethany Commandery, No.17, Knights Templars, and the Grecian Lodge, each of which met in Saunders Hall on Essex Street when this photograph was taken *c.* 1919.

Like those attending most Sunday schools in 1947, children of the Third Baptist Church on Tower Hill were expected to be punctual and dressed in proper attire. From left to right are as follows: (front row) Ernestine Murphy, Patty Jones, Larry Perry, Claude Brown, Ron Faust, Marcia Brown, Ralph Murphy Jr., and Catherine Smith; (middle row) Arthur Ward Jr., John Brown Jr., George Jones Jr., James Murphy, Barbara Brown, Sandra Perry, Fannie Murphy, Reverend Julius Mitchell, and Walter Green; (back row) Bill Perry, Dick Ward, and Dana McIlwain.

"A sound mind in a sound body," was the motto of the German Turner movement. Stressing health, physical education, and the arts, the Turners were also a political movement. Once extremely popular, the Lawrence Turn Verein originated in a house on Union Street. Gymnastics was the group's first sport. Its eventual home was Turn Hall on Park Street, where these young women were photographed c. 1913. The building still stands.

Cold weather fun like sledding down Bodwell Street c. 1895 was far more feasible on uncluttered streets than it is today. Winter carnivals, especially those in the 1920s held on the "lightning coast"—a hill above Riley Park in South Lawrence—were very well attended and often included beauty contests. Actress Thelma Todd won one during her school days here. Such improbable-sounding and risky escapades as horseracing atop the frozen Merrimack River were also not uncommon.

The Vocalaires were a diversified group of amateur singers from the Greater Lawrence area formed in the 1950s by director Edward Comtois (front row, first on the left). Patterned after Fred Waring's Pennsylvanians, the Vocalaires also sang spirituals and traditional American songs like the "Battle Hymn of the Republic," which they performed on the Major Bowes radio show in Boston. Featured regularly on Lawrence's WLAW Radio, their signature song was "Blue Skies."

Volunteering to sell war bonds during the two world wars was a civic duty similar to other war work on the home front. Occasionally celebrities like Jimmy Stewart (second from left), seen here c. 1942, arrived for monster rallies. The others in this photograph are, from left to right, Frank Capra (who directed Stewart in such films as *It's a Wonderful Life*), Herbert Thomas of the *Eagle Tribune*, Joe Liss of the Palace Theater, and John O'Hearn and John Doherty of the *Eagle Tribune*.

A supervised playground movement originated in the summer of 1912. Instructors were hired to teach children exercise and useful hobbies in the city's parks. By 1922 this swimming pool was constructed on the corner of Marion Avenue and Hampshire Street behind the county jail. Designed by architect James Allen, the Ward 4 pool (later the Kennedy Playstead) was the first in the city, costing $40,000 to build. Although the pool was a success for years, Central Catholic High School occupies this site today.

Memorial Day parades were much-anticipated events ever since the holiday was first recognized as a national day of remembrance following the Civil War. The parades drew thousands of onlookers and attracted hundreds of participants. This 1906 parade, proceeding down Manchester Street past the Arlington Mills dye house, is on its way to Bellevue Cemetery.

The Irish initiated St. Patrick's Day parades in 1864, becoming the first immigrant group to march in celebration of their ethnicity.

Lawrencians embraced the game of baseball in its early days. Found among the oldest surviving baseball cards in America are images of Lawrence men. Amateur teams were sponsored by mills, retailers, clubs, saloons, churches, and schools. The city also had its professional teams. Both Roy Campanella and Don Newcombe, future National League MVP's, played against the Lawrence Millionaires at O'Sullivan Park in 1946. Above, Irish and French-Canadian boys enjoy stickball on Tyler Street, c. 1901.

Little League began in Lawrence at O'Sullivan Park in the early 1950s with WCCM Radio covering the games. Shown here are the Lawrence Kiwanis Little League Champions for 1951. From left to right are as follows: (front row) John Hickey and James Schaake; (middle row) Jim Sullivan, John DiBenedetto, John Kennedy, Bob Lippe, Dave Tozier, John Barrett Jr., Mike Manzi, Jim Jordan, and Larry Halloran; (back row) George Driscoll, Joe Barrett, Dave Kiernan, Joe Conley, Bob Zolubos, Maurice Ferris, John McParland, Jim Murphy, and Pete McParland.

Eleven teams competed in the Massachusetts Police League for the 1914 season. Among them was this Lawrence team, composed entirely of active officers. Games began by 11 am so that police on night duty could play. A number of these Lawrence men had also played semi-pro ball. From left to right are as follows: (front row) Duhamel, Berthel, and Ahern; (middle row) McDonald, Barry, McKenna, Cadogen, and Gallagher; (back row) Kilpatrick, Murray, Hewitt, Carey, Young, and Lavin.

In 1958 the Holihans, Greater Lawrence Park League Softball Champions, drew ten thousand fans to witness their defeat of Raytheon in four of five games at the Hayden-Schofield Playstead. From left to right are as follows: (front row) Angie Robito, Jimmy Reusch, Jack Dean, and Joe Lee; (second row) Tony Puglisi, Tom Ruffen, Charles Fiorino, and Joe Carter; (third row) Frank Picone, Ray Lynch, Joe Morgan, and Billy Ford; (back row) manager Leo McCarthy, unknown, and Phil Corriveau.

Central Catholic High School began its great basketball tradition in 1936. An especially productive period for CCHS was the 1950s, when they were part of the Greater Boston Catholic League, playing teams like Matignon, Malden Catholic, and St. John's Prep. This 1958 varsity team went 23–2 for their season. From left to right are the following: (front row) captain Regan, Lacharite, Myskowski, Brother Timothy Gerard, Damphouse, Baddour, and Stopyra; (back row) Koza, Bleczinski, Courtemanche, McCarthy, and Maheu.

For earlier generations, like these prodigies c. 1913, learning to play musical instruments was more than just a great accomplishment. The skill contributed to being considered a cultured individual. Thus countless after-school and weekend hours were devoted to musical pursuits. Occasionally greatness emerged. Renowned composer George Whitefield Chadwick brought distinction to Lawrence. Davis Shuman, a Russian Jew from the Arlington district, played with the Pittsburgh Symphony Orchestra and later invented both the angular trombone and the angel trumpet.

These boys look suspiciously like they've just been caught preparing for an intense game of stickball, having replaced the ball with a crumpled newspaper about to be ignited with an unseen incendiary device. Taken around 1917, this photograph shows the alley behind the old Central Fire Station on Lowell Street.

Like many street games, the favorites were often dangerous to say nothing of illegal. Others, like quoits, horseshoes, marbles, mumblety-peg, and flying kites were ordinary diversions. For a smile blacksmith Frank O'Brien, on the corner of Carver and Salem Streets, would give any kid old horseshoes free.

Until pollution and neglect discouraged public use, water sports drew much attention to the Merrimack River. The Lawrence Canoe Club's war canoe team is pictured above the Great Stone Dam in 1920. Having set a new world's record for a mile race that year, the team consisted of Chris Lynch, Fred Koch, Al Roy, Fred Speed, Dan Murray, Fred Henning, Elmer Parker, Forrest Butland, and Art Simmers. This war canoe remains on display in the Beshara Boat House on Eaton Place.

Kinder-Theater

in der

Turn-Halle,

Sonntag, 5. Januar 1913.

Zur Aufführung gelangt:

„Wilhelm Tell".

Schauspiel in fünf Akten von Ernst Siewert.

Personen:

Hermann Geßler, Reichsvogt in Schwyz und Uri,	Alfred Hildebrandt
Werner Stauffacher, } Landleute aus Schwyz	Julius Lafferi
Konrad Hunn,	Herbert Kocher
Walter Fürst,	Herbert Grieß
Wilhelm Tell, } Landleute aus Uri,	Ernst Leyold
Kuoni, der Hirt,	Herm. Schneider
Ruodi, der Fischer,	Arthur Hilbert
Arnold Melchthal, } Landleute aus Unterwalden,	Karl Toepler
Konrad Baumgarten	Gustav Läffig
Leuthold, Hauptmann der Söldner,	Hermann Liehling
Hedwig, Tells Gattin,	Bertha Naese
Walter, } Tells Kinder,	Julius Emmert
Wilhelm,	Clemens Emmert

Söldner, Landler :c aus den Waldstätten.

Anfang 7½ Uhr.

Um zahlreichen Besuch bittet   Das Vergnügungs-Komite.

Ernst Siewert's five-act play, *William Tell*, received a spirited interpretation in this children's theater production performed on January 5, 1913, at Turn Hall. All of the children appearing on this playbill were local residents.

Ethnic theater, whether sponsored by churches, schools, clubs, or other social organizations, drew big crowds. These theatricals were generally traditional dramas familiar to a particular immigrant group. Ethnic theater assured that yet another generation removed from the old country would be exposed to the language and legend of that nationality. Besides, it was fun.

Ethnic social clubs were a refuge and link in the American communities. Offering kinship and information, many of these clubs also encouraged citizenship. In 1915, French-Canadians initiated the French Social Naturalization Club, which continues today. Here in 1962, members celebrate their heritage with Rose Kennedy, the president's mother, at their hall on Lowell Street. Mrs. Kennedy is seated at the head table, ninth from the right. The club now meets on Broadway in a new building.

By the 1890s, cycling became a formidable sport in this city much as it had in the rest of the country. Lawrence's first bicycle club was established in 1880. With the introduction of the Victor Safety Bicycle in the late 1880s, women quickly became enthusiasts of this initially expensive sport. Although racing was preeminent in most clubs, touring was also popular. Members of the Lawrence Wheelmen's Club gather on a still undeveloped portion of Andover Street at the foot of Carleton Street in 1895.

Saturday afternoons in winter were the busiest times in Moe's Pool Room at 85 Newbury Street. Games cost 5¢. Bets were usually 5¢ a ball, except on Saturdays when bets could reach 25¢. The most popular games were 8-ball, straight pool, 61-ball, and 9-ball. When this 1946 photograph was shot, only men played pool here. From left to right are Joe Alaimo, Willie Pappalardo, Fred Maccarone, Al Tucci, Jim Misserville, Don Nicolosi, "Ferdinand," Moe Zappala (owner), and Steve Leone.

As these Immaculate Conception lettermen eagerly demonstrate *c.* 1907, the manly art of boxing thrived in the Immigrant City. The Irish who helped build the dam probably staged the first matches. Since then the tradition has carried on, embracing most nationalities. Andy Callahan, Kloby Corcoran, Art Flynn, Maurice Despres, Al Mello, Nick Maloof, Joe Nantonis, and Dick Sarkis are but a few memorable champs.

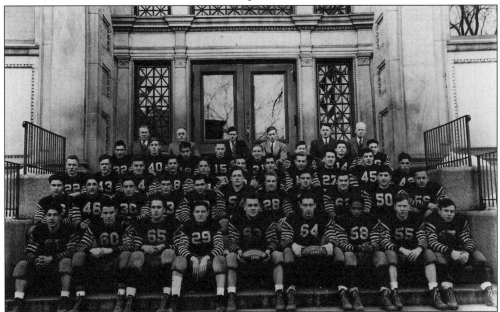

Football players at Lawrence High School have been in uniform since the year 1880. Athletes bought their own uniforms consisting of only two pieces: a rough canvas jacket and knitted pants. No helmets. No padding. No mouthguards. Maybe a knit cap. When Lawrence played Phillips Academy that year, the team walked to Andover and back, humiliated! They had been shut out. A considerably improved 1940–41 team sits with Coach Mark Devlin (top row, far right), who once played with the legendary Jim Thorpe.

The year 1948 was only the second in the history of Lawrence High that an all-female cheerleading squad represented the school. As this photograph was being shot, the administration was still uncertain if this was such a good idea. From left to right are as follows: (front row) Elaine Somers, captain Joan Balezentes, and Alice Dudash; (back row) Helen Petroccione, Gloria Chakurmanian, Arlene Devine, Joan Lynch, Ann Smith, Marie Garvey, Marilyn Golan, and Barbara Hildebrandt.

Roland Russell, Val Jean, Frankie Kahn, and Tony Brown were the most celebrated Lawrence dance bands of the '40s and '50s. Among the choice musical hotspots then were Turn Hall, the Hofbrau, St. Mary's Ballroom, Truell Hall, the Recreation Ballroom, and the Lawrence Canoe Club. Neighboring Roseland and Merrimack Park in Methuen, the Balmoral Spa in Shawsheen, and Canobie Lake Park in Salem, New Hampshire, were also favorites. Pianist Tony Brown stands with his orchestra c. 1943 in the Winnipesaukee Gardens at Weirs Beach.

LAWRENCE
Riding Park,
LAWRENCE, MASS.

＊ ＊ ＊ ＊ ＊ ＊

＊JUNE＊

17 and 18,

1896.

＊ ＊ ＊ ＊ ＊ ＊

SKINNER & HEROUX,

LESSEES,

Until the 1920s, what is now Veterans Memorial Stadium was the Lawrence Riding Park. Originally a 20-acre site, this riding or driving park with private racetrack was laid out long before there was development in this section of South Lawrence.

Horseracing was never foreign to Lawrencians. South Broadway from Shattuck to what is now Inman Street was once a celebrated Saturday racetrack. According to this 1896 racing program, pacers and trotters competed at the riding park for purses totaling $300 in mid-week races. In the 1920s the city purchased all the land for about $300,000—Veterans Memorial Park was dedicated in October 1926.

John McDuffie of North Andover prepares to race his horse, Julius De Forest, on Salem Street c. 1920 opposite the South Common. Behind him is Lawrence horse trader Tom McDonnell, who ran an auction stable on Carver Street. Racing on Salem Street (an early cement road) from Parker to South Union Streets was often a regular feature of Saturday and Sunday mornings from around 1906 into the 1920s. Although the racing was legal, it was the illicit gambling that kept things interesting.

Members of L'Union St. Jean-Baptiste staged plays and concerts to support the aims of their organization for Catholic mutual aid. Associations like these were established in French-Canadian enclaves to perpetuate and disseminate the French language through drama and song, preserve the Catholic faith, safeguard immigrant rights, and provide insurance to those unable to purchase it elsewhere. This play, *A Celebrated Case*, was well attended. Most of these performers were also local workers who worshipped at St. Anne's.

Barbara Ruth Roberts was required to learn French for her ballet classes at the Gingras School of Dance. The Gingras sisters taught the French art of ballet in their Essex Street home and expected students to understand French for their routines. Barbara was about twelve years old when this *c.* 1932 photograph was shot. Her mother, a finish mender in the Washington Mill, frequently made her costumes like the one she is wearing here.

Gingras students were considered among the most disciplined and best-trained dancers in New England. The sisters retired in 1962.

Ethnic music was often heard live on the weekends when radio stations like Lawrence's WLAW broadcast a variety of local talent. The Polka Dots, *c.* 1941, were among the early bands to play regularly on the radio. Composed of Lawrence musicians, the group specialized in polka music, which boasted a large following. From left to right are Joe Dziadosz (band leader, violin), Chris Kelley (drums), Joe Blezinski (guitar), Carl Thomas (sax), Joe Rejewski (accordion), Ray Camire (clarinet), Bill Soslovitch (banjo), and Bill Stanley (sax).

Organized in 1886 on Prospect Hill, the Concordia Club originated as both a social and shooting club for German men. Germans regularly celebrated "Schuetzenfest," a traditional festival highlighting target shooting and guncraft. Dancing, parades, and concerts were often a part of the event. Concordia marksmen pose atop Prospect Hill c. 1905. Although it continues today only as a social club, Concordia membership is open to all nationalities.

Immigrants from Mushgura, Lebanon, pose for a group shot at a Methuen campground c. 1915. Each of these adults emigrated to the Lawrence area between the 1890s and World War I. First-generation immigrants from the same villages frequently gathered to share news and gossip. Among the choice locations were their ethnic cemeteries. Members of the Hajjar and Batal families are represented above. This photograph also hangs as part of the permanent exhibit at the Ellis Island Museum.

Bowling was popular among early settlers, who usually enjoyed beer and oysters with their strikes and spares. By the 1920s there were nine different bowling alleys in the city: four on Essex Street, two on Broadway, and one each on Common, Hampshire, and Park Streets. Alleys featured professional bowl-a-thons with twenty-string matches between two players for a purse of maybe $200 a night!

Lawrencians favored duckpins over candlepins. This 1925–26 New England Championship team from the Transfer Alleys at 575A Essex Street was composed of, from left to right, as follows: (seated) John Tanzer, Joe Thomas, and John Fyfe; (standing) Jim Ross, Nick Carter, Jim Gillette, and Herb Chamberlain.

For Scottish folk in the city, no date was imbued with more significance than January 25, the birthday of the Scottish national poet, Robert Burns, in 1759. Commemorated yearly with much festivity, the event was also a celebration of Scottish heritage. Parishioners of the First United Presbyterian Church donned tartans and kilts *c.* 1942 for "A Night with Robert Burns," whose portrait hangs above them. Minister Archibald Macmillan sits in the middle row, third from the left, next to organist Grace Innes (at right).

The 4 miles that constituted Salisbury Beach in 1911 were an attraction to young Lawrence mill workers like these on holiday. From main offices in the Bay State Building, the Salisbury Associates promoted this recently purchased seacoast development by offering visitors, "a granolithic walk eight and one-half feet wide along the Beach front." Some choice lots with "suitable restrictions" sold for $200. Trolleys made the nearly three-hour ride—one way—for about 50¢.

At attention on the steps of Holy Trinity Church on Easter Sunday 1914 are youthful members of the Polish Falcons, a fraternal society, with their local priest, Father Wojtanowski. The Falcons originated among Slavs in nineteenth-century Europe. Similar in certain respects to the German Turners, the Falcons emphasized Polish nationalism, strength through fitness, and fraternalism. By the time this picture was taken, World War I had just begun overseas.

Arabic men devoted a considerable portion of their free time to philanthropic causes. The Cedar Club, an organization of Lebanese males shown here outside the club's 10 Lowell Street home *c.* 1945, was formed in the 1920s as an offshoot of the Marionite Ladies Aid Society. Besides offering charitable support to members, the group assisted in the development of St. Anthony's Marionite Church and St. George's Orthodox Church, the oldest orthodox church in the United States. Classes in Arabic were also offered by the club.

Members are, from left to right, as follows: (front row) Bill Kalil, Nick Azzi, Charles Khoury, Habib Gabour, Mansour Khoury, Abdo Kalil, and Charles Touma; (middle row) Assad Kalil, John Habib, Majeed Nassif, Elias Gabriel, Beshara Coorey, Mansour Ameen, Jacob Eyssi, Assad Phnsoka, Masoud Salem, Nick Salem, Joe Salem, and Saleem Nackly; (back row) Antoon Abdoo, Michael Gabriel, Mansour John, Habib Nackley, Abdo Mansour, Charles Azzi, Najib Khoury, Nick Khoury, Hassan Salem, Joe Khoury, Ned Daher, and Joe Daher.

Five
Essex Street Revisited

Essex Street, the principal business thoroughfare, was built up rapidly on the north side from Newbury to Amesbury Street. In 1846, at the first public sale of land, a parcel on the corner of Jackson and Essex Street was the most prized.

Initially, structures on Essex Street were temporary, built mostly of wood. However, the Essex Company, ever concerned with the danger of fire, soon required new construction to be of stone, brick, or iron. Buildings had to be at least three stories with roofs of metal or slate. Most of these permanent buildings were designed with a first floor for conducting business, a second floor for offices, and third and fourth floors to be rented for living quarters.

Here, looking west from Jackson to Lawrence Street in 1893, is a view of what was the busiest section of Essex Street.

A block of wooden structures occupied this site on the northeast corner of Essex Street and Broadway until the Meigs Building, seen here, was erected during World War I. Originally owned by Carrie Meigs, this two-story brick edifice contained a central entrance leading to second-floor offices, while at street level various commercial enterprises were housed. The photograph above was taken before urban renewal destroyed the building in the 1970s. The eight-story Essex Towers apartments are situated here.

Finish carpenter Alexander Vanasse sits for a shoeshine at Luigi Marcello's Bay State Boot Black Parlor in the basement of the Bay State Building c. 1923. In the background, sharing space with Marcello's operation, is Jim Ashburn's Barber Shop. A popular expression of the day conceded that, "nothing says more about a man's appearance than his shoes."

Although various bootblacks followed in other locations in subsequent years, the Bay State Building continued to be a favorite spot on Essex Street for gentlemen to receive a daily shine.

Norcross & Currier were probably Lawrence's first photographers, maintaining a daguerrian studio at No. 2 Merchant's Row on Essex Street in 1846. With few exceptions, photographers were located on Essex Street in the nineteenth century. Martin W. Mealey ran this studio at 411 Essex Street in 1871, selling picture frames and birdcages too. Small, framed portrait photographs are shown on the outside wall. Mealey departed for Colorado in 1881. Later, this became the location of Little Town Toggery.

Bill posting was primarily a nocturnal occupation performed after midnight when there were few interruptions and workers could move around freely. Essex Street was the prime target of these paste brigades. Sheets of advertising matter were pasted on billboards, walls, and fences, announcing theatrical attractions, land sales, circuses, ship arrivals and departures, auctions, political items, and consumer goods. This *c.* 1870 photomontage is a good example of innovative cooperative advertising between Mealey the photographer and Baker the adman.

Tuesdays, Fridays, and Saturdays were the busiest shopping days on Essex Street. By the 1940s, most stores remained open until 9 pm on Tuesday and Saturday nights. Shopping patterns were determined largely by when people got paid. In the nineteenth century, mills generally paid workers monthly, but each mill did so at different times of the month. By the twentieth century, patterns changed as employees began receiving weekly paychecks. Here friends meet while window shopping at S.S. Kresge's on Essex Street around 1960.

S.S. Kresge & Co. opened a 5-10-25¢ store at 343 Essex Street in 1911 that remained until 1963. The company inaugurated a 25¢–$1.00 store at 483 Essex Street in 1922, which closed in 1936. Kresge distinguished its department stores by using a red banner for the five-and-dimes and a green one for their upscale alternative.

Sales clerks in the music department at 343 Essex Street are shown here gathered for a group shot c. 1919.

Billed as the Delmonico's of Lawrence, there was no place quite like the distinctively male and Bavarian Boehm's Cafe at 78 Essex Street. Founded in 1889 by German immigrant Adolph Boehm, the restaurant and cafe developed a prized reputation for oversized broiled lobsters and plank steaks.

In his 1955 short story, "Venite Adoremus," the distinguished American writer John McNulty, a Lawrence native, recalled playing the piano as a youth at Christmastime in "Baym's" (correct pronunciation) for $24 a week!

Oswald Boehm, who succeeded his father in 1907, sought out the "automobilist" trade, and the restaurant became one of the first local dining establishments to attract a motoring public.

Although Prohibition saw the end of Boehm's Cafe, the building lasted until the 1950s, when it made way for a Firestone Tire store.

Below, free lunch is served at Boehm's Cafe *c.* 1905.

Looking westerly from the intersection of Essex and Lawrence Streets, this spectacular *c.* 1885 photograph by O.A. Kenefick shows firefighters testing an extension ladder near the clock tower of the Odd Fellow's Building, then the tallest structure on Essex Street. Constructed in 1875, it survived modifications until a 1941 fire destroyed the building.

The open space beyond was filled in later years by the Central Building. In the background is the Romanesque-style Lawrence Opera House, which contained a first-class entertainment hall and circular balcony on its top two floors while a train station occupied the ground level. Built by the Boston & Lowell Railroad from 1878 to 1880, this was considered the most ornamental building in the city. Following World War I, it became the Rialto Theater and then the Winter Garden Auditorium.

The last passenger train departed here in 1923. The building, deemed a hazard, was demolished by the 1940s.

Lawrence's most destructive fire of 1897 occurred in the early morning hours of March 22 at 340 Essex Street in the six-year-old, six-story Gleason Building. At the time of its construction, this was the largest building in the city and contained the first hydraulic passenger elevator. The blaze originated in the basement and was discovered by night patrolman Charles Vose. Five fire department steamers could not control the blaze. Except for the facade and center wall, the structure was gutted. Although there was no loss of life, eight adults were seriously injured. Some were forced to leap out of windows to save their lives.

In this *c.* 1942 view of Essex Street looking east from Amesbury Street to Lawrence Street, the impressive Gleason Building towers above all but the Bay State Building in the background. Designed by Boston architect Arthur Gray, adapting brick and brownstone in the Richardson Romanesque style, the Gleason was built by local dry goods merchant William Oswald in 1891. Although intended primarily for commercial use, at the time of the 1897 fire it also served as living quarters for a number of residents.

By the time owner John Moeckel was assisting these unidentified women c. 1960, George Lord & Son at 445 Essex Street was the oldest locally owned shoe store in Lawrence. Founded in 1869, the store saw three generations of the Lord family grow up. Moeckel purchased the firm in 1957. By 1962 the store was in enlarged quarters at 275 Essex Street, where it remained until it ceased operations in the early 1980s.

When people think of Essex Street, they remember shopping downtown from Broadway to Union Street. But Essex Street extends over Tower Hill to Riverside Drive. In this c. 1940 aerial view, Essex Street is almost at center running east from above Margin Street past Broadway. Immediately at right is the massive Lawrence Lumber Company yard, now a shopping center. The blocks at left bounded by Essex, Margin, and Melvin Streets are where the Merrimack Courts were built in 1942.

This too was Essex Street. Prior to the 1870s, Essex Street ran only to Margin Street, where it encountered a precipice composed of soft sand and gravel called Gale's Hill. In 1876 a cut was made through the hill, which led to the extension of Essex Street. However, Gale's Hill was not leveled until the 1890s. This c. 1890 photograph shows the Greenwood Street Bridge, which extended over Essex Street (seen in the middle) until the incline was reduced to its present height.

Among caterers in the 1920s and '30s, Weigel was king. Born in Glaugau, Saxony, Alfred P. Weigel, standing first at left, emigrated to the U.S. with his parents in 1879. Growing up in Lawrence, Weigel worked up from cook to chef before choosing a career as a caterer, running Weigel's Catering Kitchen at 193 Essex Street. Keeping a hand in the kitchen was a Weigel trademark. Before his death in 1952, Weigel also attained wide recognition as a restaurateur.

"Pennies From Heaven" was the Round Robin's signature song in the 1940s. As Lawrence's "most intimate nightspot" at 416 Essex Street, between Hampshire and Amesbury Streets, Tom and Mae Reynolds' establishment featured nightly floorshows, dancing, and a fashionable men's bar.

All-star novelty shows with Danny Creedan, Jack Lidell, and Happy Richards were well-received by servicemen. The Round Robin began serving in the late 1930s, surviving into the early '50s. Foley's, the Sunshine Cafe, Cassidy's, and the Emerald Tavern were all favorite Essex Street watering holes during World War II.

An English sausagemaker named Peter Reeves first introduced Lawrencians to tomato sausage in the 1890s.

Standing first at left in this c. 1893 photograph of his 113 Essex Street retail store, Reeves became a sausage manufacturer producing beef, pork, tomato, and bologna sausage. Steak, ham, bacon, and pure leaf lard were sold as well. At the turn of the century, Reeves could offer customers 16 pounds of salt pork for $1. He died in 1906.

How many Lawrencians bought their first piano or took their first music lessons at Knuepfer & Dimmock?

Reinhardt Knuepfer originated his enterprise in 1896, selling music and instruments and Stanley Steamer automobiles, teaming with London-born businessman Read Dimmock in 1904.

Legend has it that Knuepfer, an accomplished violinist and piano tuner who emigrated from Germany as a child, was the first person in Lawrence to own an automobile.

Above, new pianos arrive c. 1946 at the 286 Essex Street store.

Jacob Sandler was one of three Jewish brothers who came from Krakenova, Lithuania, before the turn of the century. Though poor, Jacob successfully sold boots and shoes in Lawrence, inspiring his son Simon to establish the once-famous department store at 256 Essex Street. It is shown here in 1933, when it sold only surplus merchandise. In 1938 Simon returned to selling new shoes, expanding into the sale of luggage and leather goods. The business continued to 1978.

Built in 1909 by Maine hotelier D.F. Sullivan, the Needham Hotel at 572–576 Essex Street was designed for the accommodation of business travelers. When erected, this building was only a block away from the Boston & Maine Railroad North Station Depot and was situated on the city's busiest commercial thoroughfare. A portion of the Needham's first floor served as a trolley station waiting area for some time. This six-story lodging house featured a rathskeller, private dining rooms, hot and cold running water, steam heat, gas and electric lights, and elevator service. "Bristol" is the name currently appearing above the fourth-floor windows.

We remember the Recreation Center on Hampshire Street for bowling, but it housed one of the premier ballrooms in New England. Built off Essex Street in 1929 as a combination bowling alley and dance hall, the Rec opened with bowling on the first floor and dancing on the second with groups like the fourteen-member Cliff Evans Band (above). A 1941 fire damaged the second-floor promenade, which was replaced with duckpin lanes. The Rec's billiard room was a big draw on its own.

When Ernest and Irene Morin moved their busy restaurant from 364 to 291 Essex Street in the spring of 1930, the Great Depression was just a few months old. Over a hundred eateries were thriving in Lawrence with more than a dozen on Essex Street.

Founded in 1922 as a candy store at 199 Broadway, by 1924 the expanding enterprise moved to 364 Essex Street near Amesbury Street, offering customers cooked meals and baked goods. The later move in 1930 put the restaurant in a four-story building once used by the *Eagle Tribune* newspaper. It was here that the Morin family developed a reputation for fine food over the next forty-seven years. Polished pastry cases, Friday's salmon pie, coffee, and pecan pie a la mode were highlights of the busiest lunch counter on Essex Street.

Orchestra leader Joe Annalori conducts the Sophisticated Swingers *c.* 1931 in the Capri Cafe, which advertised itself as "New England's most conservative nightclub."

The Capri was recognized for its exceptional Italian cuisine with a Sicilian flavor, and its white clam sauce was itself a draw. Founder and owner Louis Laudani, a.k.a. "Kid Lewis," was a lightweight boxing champion following World War I. From 1934 to 1955, Laudani ran the restaurant at 110 Essex Street at the corner of Newbury Street that excelled as an evening retreat for the family crowd.

The first concerted effort to bring shoe manufacturing to Lawrence following the great financial panic of 1857 lead to the construction of this building on the northeast corner of Franklin and Essex Streets. First called Shoe Block, then Ordway Block, it saw the manufacture of shoes by hand for Union soldiers during the Civil War. From 1909 to 1929, when this photograph originally appeared, Nelson's Five and Dime occupied the building. Many other enterprises have followed.

Designed by local architect Charles T. Emerson, Saunders Block was built on the southwest corner of Essex and Appleton Streets in the early 1870s by Daniel Saunders & Sons. It stood until the mid-1920s. Stores and offices occupied the first two floors. The top two floors consisted primarily of halls for public use. Various Masonic groups leased these halls for many years. Around 1926, the Merchants Trust Company constructed an office on a portion of this site at 238 Essex Street. It still remains, bounded by a parking lot.

Until the end of World War II, Brockelman's, Ganem's, and the Mohican were the city's biggest and busiest markets. Even before the arrival of the supermarket chains, they were the prime competitors in the downtown area for a Lawrencian's food dollar. Stanley Novick (left) and Tom Kamal (right) man the meat counter in the Mohican at 374 Essex Street in 1937. During World War II, Thursdays were famous for fresh specials.

Haggling over prices was a common practice in 1880 when R.J. Macartney arrived from Lowell to open his own clothing store on Essex Street, the Lawrence One Price Clothing Store. Macartney guaranteed "one fair price for all." In 1904 this 431 Essex Street store became known as Macartney's Apparel Shop. Urban renewal demolished the structure some sixty years later. Following expansion in 1928, the name changed again to Macartney's. In 1971, the business moved across the street into Ganem's old market. By 1990, Macartney's moved to Andover.

Among the most fashionable men's clothing stores, Macartney's employed many of the city's most knowledgeable salespeople. Leo Columbe, at left, came from Therrien's Men's Store in the early 1960s, when this picture was taken. John Choquette (right) had owned Zuber-Choate Company, quality clothiers. Each was a seasoned specialist in men's apparel working in the furnishings department. Macartney's is remembered for its balcony shoe department and as a supplier of Boy Scout attire at 431 Essex Street.

Mr. Peanut meandering up the south side of Essex Street in the fall of 1940 wasn't really such a peculiar sight. The giant prototype was the sensation of the World's Fair that year where, as the juggling host of the Planter Nut & Chocolate Company exhibit, he greeted hundreds of Lawrencians vacationing in New York.

Essex Street in the 1940s to the end of World War II sold lots of nuts. Angelina De Giovanni, Fanny Farmer, Junkins, Peters & Co., Priscilla's, D.L. Page Co., and Victory Nut all sold peanuts. The National Peanut Corporation at 400 Essex Street was the sponsor of this smiling goober with the monocle.

A casual walk down the north side of Essex Street in the spring of 1940 from Franklin to Hampshire Street might mean a stop in the photograph booth at Woolworth's before buying licorice at W.T. Grant's, or encountering some polka dot ties while rushing past Hal's Men's Shop en route to Dr. McArdle's office in the Blakeley Building. Trying on clothes at Bon Marche never could equal the excitement of window shopping with friends at Kay Jewelers on a sunny Saturday afternoon.

Located on the southeast corner of Essex and Appleton Streets are the remaining two stories of this striking commercial block at 232–236 Essex Street. Built by the German-born tailor Frederick W. Schaake from 1867 to 1869, the structure was known alternately as Schaake's Block or Post Office Block. The post office was situated here during the latter part of the nineteenth century.

A 1939 fire destroyed the mansard roof and top story. Remodeled and renamed the Appleton Building, this was the address for Elliot's, sellers of home furnishings from the 1940s to the 1970s.

A curiosity today, Dora Hall's Human Hair Store was located at left on the first floor in 1890. Miss Hall advertises herself as "sole agent for Her Majesty's Corset's," showcasing a variety of these in one display window and human hair samples in the other (wigs were a common item then, too). Tenants included the Lawrence Savings Bank, Mr. Schaake, the *Lawrence American* newspaper, and Attorney N.P. Frye of North Andover.

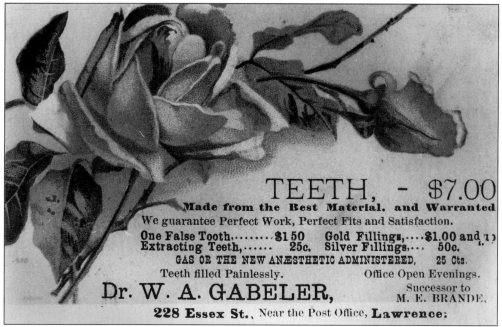

TEETH, - $7.00

Made from the Best Material, and Warranted.
We guarantee Perfect Work, Perfect Fits and Satisfaction.

One False Tooth,........$1 50   Gold Fillings,....$1.00 and 1)
Extracting Teeth,...... 25c.   Silver Fillings,... 50c.
GAS OR THE NEW ANÆSTHETIC ADMINISTERED,   25 Cts.
Teeth filled Painlessly.   Office Open Evenings.

Dr. W. A. GABELER,   Successor to
                                M. E. BRANDE.

228 Essex St., Near the Post Office, **Lawrence:**

By 1890 William Gabeler was one of fourteen dentists with offices on Essex Street. Competition was intense. Colorful trade cards like the above were offered as handouts in offices and were even distributed on the street. Gabeler succeeded Malon E. Brande at 228 Essex Street in 1888. Following a move next door to Schaake's Block in 1893, he was joined by Charles W. Lacaillade for a number of years. Gabeler's son Charles became associated with him professionally in 1914.

American heavyweight boxing champion Jim Jeffries was in town for an exhibition fight in February of 1899. He is shown here (center) leaning on the bar in the New Central Hotel at 345 Essex Street. To the right of the champ is the hotel's Irish-born proprietor R.A. Carter, sporting a mustache.

At the turn of the century this was the theater district of Lawrence with the Opera House and New Theater across the street. As this time there were no movie houses on Broadway.

Woolworth's was the first national department store chain to establish itself in Lawrence, doing so around 1899 at 275 Essex near Pemberton Street. In the early 1920s it moved to this newly renovated building with an art-deco facade on the northwest corner of Essex and Hampshire Streets. Seen here in front of the store during the early 1960s is a crowded waiting area for local buses.

Lawrencians generally refer to this as the end of Essex Street instead of the beginning, which it is. Seen from the second floor of the Essex Company's main building at number 6, Essex Street looks west to Newbury Street. The year is 1917 and these troops have just completed their duties marching in a parade. America had recently entered the war in Europe. At left, Italian flags blow in the wind atop tenements crowded with paesani who dominate this section of downtown.

Six
Gone but Not Forgotten

Steam locomotives receive service c. 1935 in the Boston & Maine Railroad roundhouse on South Union Street near the White Pups Bridge. The brick roundhouse shown above was built around 1910 to provide shelter for servicing and cleaning trains. Today much of this site is covered by the Valley Forum, a skating rink. Lawrence was a major rail center almost from its inception. In 1848 the Boston & Maine chose to race a special 10-ton steam locomotive 26 miles from Boston to Lawrence in twenty-six minutes. This became the first mile-a-minute train in American history. Like the aforementioned train and roundhouse, this chapter is devoted not only to things gone but to people, places, and events that you may not have known ever existed here.

This aerial view of downtown Lawrence as seen from atop the Upper Pacific Mills looking east was taken about ten years after the Civil War, c. 1875. It reveals the carefully planned city designed by civil engineer Charles Storrow of the Essex Company in 1845. Only a small portion of what appears here still remains.

Starting at the bottom right of the picture on the North Canal island are buildings belonging to the Atlantic Mills followed by those of the Lower Pacific Mills. The Central Bridge (not shown) was constructed here during World War I. The Moseley truss bridge spanning the canal led to Atlantic Street, which no longer exists. The dark row of trees across from the canal grow

on one side of Canal Street, while a row of Atlantic Mills boarding houses occupy the other. That small open space at the bottom left is the intersection of Canal and Hampshire Streets. A second row of boarding houses runs along Methuen Street. The open spaces to the left of those boarding houses are actually undeveloped sections of Essex Street (on the south side of the street that made up what was called the corporation reserve). Another row of trees hides some of the merchant blocks on the north side of Essex Street. The tower of city hall rises above a large wooded area that is the North Common.

During the 1850s this was the home of William C. Chapin, who was hired by Abbott Lawrence himself as resident agent for the booming Pacific Mills. In the American textile industry of the nineteenth century, mill agents were among the most powerful men in a corporation. Situated atop a then pristine Graves (now Clover) Hill, this wooden house was bounded by Pleasant (now Fern) Street and Tarbox (now Berkeley) Street. Today the site is occupied by the Berkeley Retirement Home.

This lithographic view depicts what William C. Chapin could see from his Clover Hill estate, mentioned above, in 1856. The mill complex farthest to the right in the background is Agent Chapin's Pacific Mills. To the right is the Merrimack River. That mass of smaller buildings represents Lawrence below the Spicket River, which flows across the landscape. At this time there was little detailed development from the Spicket to the base of Clover Hill. Fern Street is in the foreground.

To raise money for the United Presbyterian Church on Haverhill Street in the 1940s, an annual mock wedding was staged by young parishioners. Based on the actual marriage ceremony of P.T. Barnum's famous adult midgets, Tom Thumb (3 feet, 4 inches) and Lavinia Warren (2 feet, 8 inches) in 1863, a Tom Thumb Wedding was recreated by these children in homemade costumes as seen here in 1946. From left to right are Gelinas, Innes, Tordoff, Gillespie, Domingue, Emery, Tordoff, MacMillan, Reinhold, Murray, Ela, Gill, Domingue, and Platt.

Macadam was the choice of city officials for paving Lawrence streets in the nineteenth century. The best stone quarried was from the Essex Company's blue ledge on Emmett Street behind the Wetherbee School. This stone crusher was moved to the site in 1893. By 1896 the crusher ran from February to December, producing 25,000 tons of stone for the city's thoroughfares. The crusher remained operative into the twentieth century until excavation was no longer cost-effective.

At the time of his death in 1982, one local paper called him "Lawrence's most curious native son."

Born Ferdinand Waldo Demara Jr. in 1921, he became known as "The Great Imposter" after he was the subject of a book and film with this title in the late 1950s. His amazing exploits, usually conducted under assumed identities, fascinated Americans.

Seen standing to the right of Brother Joannes, Demara attended Central Catholic High School in the 1930s. It was while masquerading as a clergyman and performing good works that he would achieve what little satisfaction he could out of a life that in the end he called a failure.

An English-born cotton manufacturer named Thomas Greenbank had this substantial house shipped in sections from Gaysville, Vermont, in 1873. Greenbank, whose mill on the South Canal had just been built, was settling here. This is Bailey Street in South Lawrence around 1895. In the background is the Parker Street Methodist Episcopal Church. At the far left the chimneys of the Parker Street School can be seen. Today, this corner is home to the South Lawrence Library, which opened in 1927.

Among the earliest Protestant societies to form in Lawrence was the First Baptist Church, whose members began services around 1847 in their homes.

From 1849 to 1850 this impressive edifice, shown c. 1897, was erected at the southeast corner of Amesbury and Haverhill Streets on land donated by the Essex Company. In 1859 the Reverend J. Sella Martin, a former slave, preached here for some time.

On the day after Christmas in 1933, during the worst snowstorm of the season, this entire wooden structure was destroyed in an electrical fire. The Salvation Army currently maintains offices in a new building on this site.

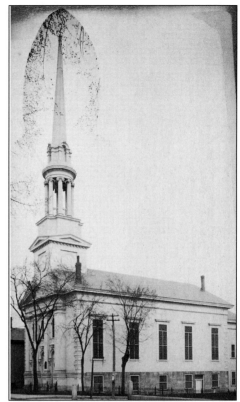

In the 1930s Lawrence's vibrant Jewish community supported four synagogues in the heart of the city. A common meeting place for their members and children was the Young Men's Hebrew Association building at 46–48 Concord Street, which served as the Jewish Community Center from the 1930s to the 1950s. Originally a church, the structure was remodeled in 1937 to provide an auditorium, stage, kitchens, and meeting rooms. Vacated in the late '50s, it was demolished in the 1960s.

Route 114 coming into Lawrence from North Andover looked like this in 1893. Called the Salem Turnpike, this was an old, established coaching road that became a prime access route for the delivery of goods from the Salem seaport to the growing communities of northern Essex County. This bridge is opposite Den Rock Park. Costs to repair it and another South Lawrence bridge in 1890 amounted to $1.75. Substantially more traffic passes over the concrete bridge that is there today over the Shawsheen River.

Motion picture actress Thelma Todd (crouched above in 1931), a Lawrence native, was born on July 26, 1905. She graduated from Lawrence High School in 1923. A natural blond, Thelma was a beauty queen who gave up thoughts of becoming a teacher to pursue a film career. Her first pictures were silent movies. A talented comedienne, she starred in sound films with Laurel and Hardy, the Marx Brothers, and Gary Cooper. Her suspicious death in 1935 remains one of Hollywood's great unsolved mysteries.

110

Lawrence's Johnny Broaca, wearing glasses, sits between the legendary Lou Gehrig, at left, and Joltin' Joe DiMaggio, at right, as a member of the World Champion 1936 New York Yankees. The son of a Lithuanian immigrant mill worker, Johnny was born in 1910. Known for his fastball, in 1934 he pitched his rookie season with the Yankees. However, his baseball career was short-lived. By 1939 Broaca was back at his Garden Street home, where he lived until his death in 1985.

If you stood at the southeast corner of Broadway and Canal Streets near Lawton's Frankfurt Stand today, you would probably have a difficult time believing that this is Canal Street. But not in 1890. Then, at left, were the boarding houses of the Pacific Mills, which were replaced by company mill buildings in later years. At right is the North Canal and the gigantic Upper Pacific Mills. Virtually everything in this view is now gone.

The Pulitzer-prize-winning poet Robert Frost was born on March 26, 1874, in San Francisco. Upon the death of his father he came to Lawrence to live with relatives. Frost began publishing poetry in the *Lawrence High School Bulletin*. Upon graduation in 1892, when this photograph was taken, he was co-valedictorian with his future wife, Eleanor White. Following a brief college experience, Frost worked in Greater Lawrence and in southern New Hampshire until he sailed to England in 1912. In 1925 he recalled, "One of the great books that I came near writing but which I didn't write was the history of Lawrence." Frost returned to Lawrence for the dedication of the Robert Lee Frost School in 1962 and died in 1963.

Known to generations of Lawrencians as the Parker Manor on the northeast corner of Lawrence and Haverhill Streets, this building was replaced by the new Lawrence Public Library in the 1970s. The Pacific Mills owned this lot since the nineteenth century. It is not unlikely that the mansion, shown in 1893, was built for Walter E. Parker, agent of the Pacific Mills from 1892 to 1924. Following his retirement the building became a lodging house.

The New Nickel Theatre, Lawrence, Mass.

The original Nickel Theater on the northeast corner of Lawrence and Methuen Streets opened in 1906. This was a theater previously known as the Casto, located above Porter's livery stable. By February of 1907 the Nickel offered continuous performances of "moving pictures and illustrated songs" for 5¢ daily from 2 to 10:30 pm. The Nickel was replaced by the New Nickel Theater, which was built on the same site in 1910.

By 1915, with the continued success of film, the Empire Theater was built by the Toomey & Demara Amusement Company, replacing the New Nickel Theater. Seating 2,300, the Empire became the largest movie house in Lawrence. Local filmmaker Rosario Contarino exhibited his Methuen-made feature film, *Tangled Hearts*, here in 1924. When Warner Brothers leased the Empire in the 1930s, this became the Warner Theater, featuring motion pictures until the 1970s, when it was demolished for a bank's parking lot.

Scrap drives were a big part of the war effort on the home front in the 1940s. This crew at 2 Shattuck Street in South Lawrence did its bit. Jimmy Rylye, at the far left, even contributed his scooter to this 1942 drive. Like his little sister Eleanor, in front, he collected pots and pans with the other neighborhood children, who sometimes pooled their bubble gum to send to our boys overseas.

The only octagonal house known to have existed in nineteenth-century Lawrence belonged to General John Gale, atop the hill in Ward 5 bearing his name. Gale, a talented carriage maker from Salisbury, established a prominent factory at 256 Lowell Street in the 1850s. His rank derived from an appointment in the New Hampshire militia.

Situated on Greenwood Street, the house was midway between Essex and Lowell Streets. By the time the hill was excavated in the 1890s the house was gone.

Opposite Memorial Stadium at 75 Winthrop Avenue, the Yankee Doodle was among the most highly recommended restaurants in South Lawrence from the mid-1940s to 1973. Eaton's Restaurant preceded it, operating from 1934 to 1944. Before that Mrs. Marie Carr's Lunchroom was located here.

Into the first quarter of the twentieth century this was the far edge of development in the South Lawrence area traversed by Route 114, the old Salem Turnpike. Fires plagued this site in the 1960s and '70s. The Cactus Restaurant and Discotheque was destroyed by a fast moving blaze in 1978. Wendy's Old Fashioned Hamburgers currently resides at this address.

Below, Agnes and David Marquis Sr., a South Lawrence couple of French-Canadian heritage, celebrate a wedding anniversary surrounded by their children and grandchildren in the mid-1950s. The Yankee Doodle accommodated large groups. Its trademark entrance canopy offered a perfect opportunity for guests to capture special occasions on film.

Born at Lawrence General Hospital on August 25, 1918, to Jennie and Samuel Bernstein of Juniper Street, this musically gifted son of Russian Jewish immigrants remained in Lawrence only a few months. Leonard Bernstein, celebrated composer, spent his childhood in the Boston area, returning as an adult but once to Lawrence in 1983 for a 65th birthday celebration.

Both his mother and father had been Lawrence mill workers during the 1912 strike. The city was a good place for young Jews then with two synagogues, a shul, a shtetel, Yiddish classes, and a growing economy.

Bernstein died in New York in 1990.

Surreal in appearance, this image of the Farwell Bleachery, at right on the South Canal, was taken around 1893. Planned for textile bleaching and dying, the N.H. Farwell & Son factory was an Italianate building designed by Maine architects Stevens & Coombs in 1876. Operations began on January 1, 1878. When the Central Bridge was under construction during World War I, a significant portion of the mill was razed. Plycraft, Inc. owned the property when it was devastated by arson in 1994.

Situated on the northwest corner of Appleton and Methuen Streets was the Eliot Congregational Church, dedicated in 1866. An outgrowth of the Lawrence Street Congregational Church and the Central Congregational Church, it was named for the Colonial missionary John Eliot. In 1884 the structure was substantially altered inside, serving as the YMCA until 1909. It was then purchased by the Lawrence Gas Company, which replaced the building in the 1920s. This is now a parking lot across from Hibernian Hall.

These boys in front of the Hood School on Park Street c. 1937 were part of a national school safety program instituted by the American Automobile Association in 1920. As the number of automobiles increased, so did concern for the safety of schoolchildren. Students led these patrols, under police supervision, wearing a white sash and badge. As such, they had the authority to stop traffic. In subsequent years the program was modified in favor of adult crossing guards.

Rockefeller, Kafka, King Edward VII, and Henry James were among the disciples of this "apostle of nutrition."

Born on August 10, 1849, on Haverhill Street, Horace Fletcher, seen here around 1906, was a precocious child who left home at age sixteen. He was at various times an importer, sharpshooter, artist, manufacturer, inventor, author, manager of the New Orleans Opera House, and a philanthropist. Towards the end of his life, due to obesity and dyspepsia, he devised a system for chewing food slowly to maximize digestion and nutrition. Critics labeled it the "chew chew cult," but the public loved it. By the time of his death in 1919, "fletcherism" and "fletcherize" were part of the English language.

Maurice Curran and John Joyce, wholesale liquor distributors and brewers, began with a bottling and soda water company in 1877. By 1885 they had purchased this building, seen in 1959, at 433–443 Common Street for manufacturing. Following their retirement the company successfully survived Prohibition by producing a tasty ginger ale soft drink. The business lasted into the late 1950s. This block, now the site of the post office, was a victim of urban renewal in the 1960s.

Two Donovans from Lawrence who were not related to each other "discovered" two of baseball's greatest athletes.

"Patsy" Donovan, a nineteenth-century Irish immigrant, had a long career in the major leagues. As a pro scout he noticed a young Baltimore player named Babe Ruth, and recommended him to his old team, the Boston Red Sox.

William Edward Donovan, known not-so-affectionately as "Wild Bill," was born here October 13, 1876. It was as a pitcher for the Detroit Tigers, as this c. 1912 gum card illustrates, that "Wild Bill" achieved much of his fame. When Ty Cobb was playing for an obscure Southern team in 1905, Donovan brought him up to Detroit, launching his professional career.

Miville's at 44 Hampshire Street started in 1884 as a drugstore run by Narcisse Miville, a French-Canadian pharmacist. During World War II, as the drug business slowed, the pharmacy began selling sandwiches and doughnuts as a sideline. Creme pies overtook prescriptions in sales and Miville's became a full-time restaurant and bakery. Renowned baker Alphonse Cote was with the store, depicted here c. 1960, until it burned in 1968.

Constructed on land owned by the Knowles family near the corner of Andover and Beacon Streets, this was a working farm where the Knowles family sold water from their "Diamond Spring" for nearly half a century before Holihan's purchased the land and the spring in 1912 for a brewery. This Depression-era view of the main building may remind old-timers of the famous "tap room" that Holihan's made available free (beer included) for local functions. The landmark was leveled in the early 1970s to make way for the British Colonial Apartments, which remain.

From June 7 to 14, 1953, the city of Lawrence celebrated its centennial, beginning with a parade. This photograph shows an antique mail wagon on Essex Street. For seven full days and nights the city observed its anniversary with an historical spectacle, fireworks, sports, exhibits, a firemen's muster, a flower show, and block dancing, concluding with a centennial dinner. In the 1950s Lawrence was frequently promoted as "The Friendly City."

Agriculture was the predominant activity in much of the fertile areas of Methuen and Andover that were annexed to make up the town of Lawrence in 1847. South Lawrence was especially notable for its fields of grain and extensive apple orchards. Farms belonging to Phineas Gage, Joshua Thwing, Dan Merrill, and the White family encompassed a considerable portion of North Lawrence from the Spicket River west to the base of Tower Hill. There the Bodwell, Richardson, Ames, and Emery families maintained working farms.

This gentleman wielding a scythe *c.* 1873 is employed at the Emery Farm on the top of Tower Hill near the Methuen line.

BLUE SEAL FEEDS

In Business in Lawrence Since 1868

Original quarters of
H. K. Webster Company
on Island St., Lawrence
1868 to 1890

H. K. WEBSTER COMPANY

Manufacturers of Blue Seal Products

Richford, Vt.   Lawrence, Mass.

Henry Kingman Webster was a New Hampshire farm boy who traveled here in 1858. After working in a grain store and serving in the Civil War, Webster began selling horse feed in this rented mill on Island Street in 1868. He was elected mayor of Lawrence in 1881. In 1900 the company headquarters were on West Street. Blue Seal Feeds remains in the Webster family, though they haven't retained offices here since the late 1980s.

No outdoor sports arena in Lawrence is more fondly remembered for baseball, softball, or boxing than O'Sullivan Park on Water Street. Pictured in the 1940s, Jordan Street is behind the left field bleachers. The city purchased this property in 1918. The Lawrence Millionaires baseball team, and the city league, Little League, and high school teams all used the park. Jack Dempsey boxed here. Now the property is owned by the Lawrence Boys Club and their buildings occupy this field.

Glennie's milk wagons line up just over the city line on Massachusetts Avenue in North Andover c. 1906, ready for their early morning Lawrence deliveries. Founded in 1890, a dairy farm on Dale Street in North Andover was maintained by Charles D. Glennie. His was among the local dairies delivering milk directly to Lawrence homes every other day from the nineteenth century to the mid-twentieth century. In the 1940s and '50s, 90 Winthrop Avenue was the location of Glennie's Lawrence ice cream stand.

The Lambert-Morin Motor Vehicle Co.

Builders of Commercial Vehicles

Auto Repairs and Supplies

In 1912, forty-three-year-old Fred Lambert, a blacksmith, and fifty-two-year-old Joe Morin, a baker, manufactured electric trucks to order under the name Lambert-Morin at 638 Essex Street. Besides being a blacksmith, Lambert was a wheelwright and carriage maker who could turn out virtually anything on wheels. Morin used his own Lambert-Morin built truck for promotion and may have provided the capital for the duo's venture, which lasted about two years. Little else is known about the company.

This peek into the Plains area of the 1920s looks northeasterly from the intersection of Hampshire, Pine, and Oak Streets. The old Hampshire Street School is at left on the island. St. Joseph's Byzantine Catholic Church presides over this site today. Like the trolley tracks, Pine Street no longer exists. By the 1920s this section of the Plains was predominantly Lebanese, remaining so until it was razed in the 1960s by urban renewal.

Considered the dean of American composers of instrumental music, George Whitefield Chadwick spent his formative years on Tremont Street.

Born November 13, 1854, in Lowell, his parents moved to Lawrence before the Civil War. Chadwick's musical training began as an organist at various religious institutions around the common, like the Lawrence Street Congregational Church (see below).

Following a few years working at his father's Essex Street insurance office, Chadwick pursued musical studies in the Midwest and abroad. His first musical composition, an overture, had its American premier in Boston in 1880.

Chadwick was director of the New England Conservatory of Music 1897–1930. He died in 1931.

Organized in 1846, the Lawrence Street Congregational Church was built in 1848 on what old-timers later referred to as "Brimstone Corner" at the intersection of Lawrence and Haverhill Streets.

Looking north in 1913 from below the corner of Lawrence and Lowell Streets, this church seated almost a thousand members and cost in excess of $12,000 to build. On February 7, 1913, a fire totally consumed this structure. A stone church dedicated in 1915 replaced this edifice.

An author, lecturer, and educator, Irish-born Katherine O'Keefe (O'Mahoney) graduated from Lawrence High School in 1873, where she began her career. Robert Frost considered her one of his favorite teachers. She was also among the first Irish-American women to lecture in New England. Her books include *A Sketch of Catholicity in Lawrence and Vicinity* (1882) and *Famous Irishwomen* (1907).

Recognized by such diverse talents as the reformer Frances E. Willard and the Irish patriot Fanny Parnell, O'Keefe published a Sunday newspaper for Irish-American Catholics in Lawrence and conducted Irish classes here.

This youthful photograph was taken in the 1870s; O'Keefe died at her Tower Hill home in 1918.

Born in 1878, Harry L. Bradbury was clerking in a Lowell Street market before he began his commercial enterprise. The year was 1900 when, with horse and wagon, Bradbury entered the meat and provision business on Tower Hill. By 1910 he employed five clerks. His market remained on the corner of Warren Street at 414 Lowell Street for forty years. Upon his death in 1941, this was transformed into McGovern's Pharmacy.

This view of the southwest corner of Franklin and Common Streets, a commercial block, also reveals the ethnic constituency of this section of the city in 1926. Tobacconist Gedeon Parent, barber Honore Viel, and tailor Harry Boucher, all French-Canadians, shared their first-floor business space with the Moy Sing Chinese Laundry and the Lawrence Fruit and Produce Company, run by Lebanese owners Elias Hajjar and James Faris. Mrs. Henry Raymond, another French-Canadian, operated the top floors as a boardinghouse.

The Franklin Street School on the northeast corner of Franklin and Lowell Streets was a wooden two-story building constructed in 1854. The school closed c. 1935, after which the structure was used by the city until March of 1947, when it was sold to Shaheen Bros. Inc., wholesalers of fruit and produce. When this picture was taken in 1959, the company was the largest distributor of frozen foods in the Merrimack Valley. Urban renewal claimed the building in the early 1960s.

The Wirth brothers were bakers on Prospect Hill before they opened Wirth's Cafe as a restaurant at 42 Amesbury Street in 1935. Soups and daily specials became their forte. Thursday was boiled dinner day. Complete dinners cost about 50¢ and included either grape nut pudding custard or kuchen for dessert. Coffee Jell-O was a Wirth's novelty made from leftover coffee and real cream. Pat Pappalardo, a barber, bought the business in 1945. Wirth's became a culinary legend before closing in the 1970s.

Lawrencians in the 1940s, '50s, and '60s always called this the "transfer station" and never "the terminal." An earlier waiting area for trolleys was situated in the Needham Hotel on Essex Street. By the late 1930s, as buses replaced trolleys, the bus company moved to this 388 Essex Street location.

Upwards of seventy-five to one hundred people could pack this station. The buses operated from 5 am to 11:30 pm, seven days a week and 365 days a year, and the average fare in the 1940s was 5¢. Essex Street devotees may remember the lunch counter run by Mrs. Moriarty.

The Eastern Massachusetts Bus Co. sold the station in 1968. It closed soon after.

Acknowledgments

I especially wish to thank Helen Sapuppo, Elizabeth McAuliffe, Mary O'Hearn Armitage, Pauline Everson, Eileen Mele, Alfred Koch, Don Traynor, and Jack Lahey for their exceptional commitment to assisting me in both the preparation and completion of this book.

Arthur "Dude" Regan, the Sage of South Lawrence, at age ninety-six has taught me more about history than Thucydides.

I would also like to express my sincere appreciation to the following individuals, organizations, and businesses who provided either photographs or information for this volume:

AAA, Mary Ahearn, Grace Alakel, the Allston Family, Andover Books and Prints, the Andover Historical Society, Ralph Arivella Estate, the Arlington Trust Company, Dexter Arnold, Ph.D., Fred Arold, Marion Barker, Fred Barone, Jim Beauchesne, Joe Bella, the Bergeron-Micka Family, R. Bergeron, Rene Bernardin, Yadira Betances, Bider's Antiques, Thomas Blouin, Ronnie Bonsaint, Ferris Boshar, Ray Boshar, Barbara Brown, Tony Brown, Grace Busta, Sandra Cannella, Robert Castricone, Central Catholic High School, The Charles Studio, Laura Chesworth, Triestine Ciofolo, Michael Coleman, Edward Comtois, the Concordia Social Club, Edward J. Connolly, Virginia Craddock, L. Cunningham, Louis C. Cyr, Arthur Dallon, Martin C. Dallon, Rita C. Danahy, Joseph DeFillippo, Eartha Dengler, Theresa DePippo, Marie Devine, James DiLavore, Mellie Dome, Robert A. Domingue, Erin Driscoll, George Driscoll Jr., Norma Duchesne, the *Eagle Tribune*, Ray Ferris, Anthony Ferrucci, Margaret Firth, Bill Fontaine, Louise Haffner Fournier, Sandra Frechette, Thomas Galvin, Eva Pellerin Gamache, Rita Gingras, Dr. Armand Girouard, Blanche Grassello, Louise Hart, Viola Haynes, Marcel Hebbelinck, Susan Higgins, Hilda Holt, Janet Howell, Gertrude Ball Humphrey, Barbara Innes, Adeline Ippolito, Bob Joncas, Joan Lambert Joncas, Barbara Kaslow, Mary Ann Kaslow, Barbara Roberts Keating, Gary Keating, Gilbert Kellett, the Richard Kelley Family, Robert 'T. Kelley, John Kerry, Katherine Khalife, Edna Kidd, Geraldine Kirk, Ruth Lange, the Lawrence Chamber of Commerce, the Lawrence Community Development Department, Lawrence High School, Elaine Lee, Ned Leone, Steve Leone, Mary Lisauskas, Donald Look, Alice Dudash Lupton, Robert P. McCaffery, Ph.D., Beatrice Gingras McCarthy, Francis McGovern, Richard McGovern, M.D., Gardner Macartney, Grace Marad, Lee Marcinuk, Frank and Marie Martin, the Methuen Historical Society, Dr. Peter Miville, Irene Mordach, Irene Morin, Catherine Morrissette, Ernestine Murphy, Susan Muse, Evelyn Novick, Nancy Ann Oliskey, T. Page, Salvatore Pauta, Loel Poor, Alice Porst, Oscar Porst, JoAnn Raye, Bernard Reilly, Harry Richards, George W. Ricker, Magdalena Ripka, James and Norma Ryley, Quentin Sandler, Carole Scarito, William Schwartz, Ned Schwarz, Mitzi Sciandra, Douglas Seed, George Silverman, Joe Sirois, Marie Sirois, the Skulski Historical Image Collection, Mildred Wirth Snell, South Congregational Church, Mary Manzi Stewart, Amelia Stundza, Bernard Sullivan, Jim Sullivan, H.C. Tetreau, Helen Thomas, Anne Tulley, the Albert Veilleux Family, Ilona Volngus, the Wainwright Family, Genevieve and George Wall, Doris Wallwark, David J. Williamson, Marie Matthes Wirt, and the YWCA.